Empirical Hermeneutics, Interculturality, and Holy Scripture

Intercultural Biblical Hermeneutics Series

The Intercultural Biblical Hermeneutics Series is offered to Bible scholars and interested practitioners with a twofold purpose: to present the fruits of ongoing research in the new field of empirical intercultural hermeneutics, and to foster further conversation and collaboration.

Series Editors

Hans de Wit, Mary H. Schertz

Managing Editors

Annette Brill Bergstresser, Barbara Nelson Gingerich

Editorial Board

Eric Anum—Ghana
Evangeline Anderson—India
Janet Dyk—The Netherlands
Knut Holter—Norway
Werner Kahl—Germany
Edgar López—Colombia
Miranda Pillay—South Africa
John Prior—Indonesia
Daniel Schipani—USA
Fernando Segovia—USA

Monographs in the series

1. *Empirical Hermeneutics, Interculturality, and Holy Scripture,* by Hans de Wit, 2012

Empirical Hermeneutics, Interculturality, and Holy Scripture

Hans de Wit

Dom Hélder Câmara Chair
VU University Amsterdam

Intercultural
Biblical
Hermeneutics
Series

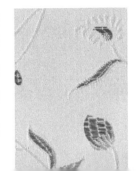

Spring 2012 | Number 1

© 2012 by Foundation Dom Hélder Câmara Chair, VU University Amsterdam.
Published in collaboration with Institute of Mennonite Studies,
3003 Benham Ave., Elkhart, Indiana 46517-1999, USA
http://www.ambs.edu/ims

Printed in the United States of America by Evangel Press, Nappanee, Indiana
Design by Annette Brill Bergstresser

The following organizations financially supported this publication:
Foundation Dom Hélder Câmara Chair; Institute of Mennonite Studies;
and Mission Department ICCO & Kerk in Actie, Protestant Church in the
Netherlands.

Unless otherwise indicated, the Scripture quotations in this monograph are from the *New Revised Standard Version Bible,* © 1989 by the Division of Christian Education of the National Council of Churches of Christ in the USA, and are used by permission.

Institute of Mennonite Studies ISBN: 0-936273-80-1

Library of Congress Cataloging-in-Publication Data

Wit, Hans de, 1949-
Empirical hermeneutics, interculturality, and Holy Scripture / Hans de Wit ; [translated from the original Dutch version by Henry Jansen].
    p. cm. -- (Intercultural biblical hermeneutics series ; spring 2012, no. 1)
Includes bibliographical references (p.   ).
ISBN 0-936273-80-1 (alk. paper)
1. Bible--Hermeneutics. 2. Bible--Reader-response criticism. 3. Multiculturalism--Religious aspects--Christianity. I. Title.
BS476.W5813 2012
220.601--dc23
                              2012014137

For Marijn, Sara, and Rebekka,
and all the memories we share

Contents

Introduction

In 1985, some years before the debate on multicultural society erupted in the Netherlands, the Colombian Nobel Prize–winning novelist Gabriel García Márquez published his novel *Love in the Time of Cholera*. This novel tells the story of the impossible love between a man and a woman, Florentino and Fermina. It is fascinating to read the novel from the perspective of culture, as it contains almost everything that one should know about intercultural communication. I will introduce the content of this monograph via a summary of this novel.

Love in the Time of Cholera

The story takes place in Colombia, somewhere in the tropical northern region on the Caribbean coast. It is the beginning of the twentieth century. Florentino, an illegitimate son—a product of a fleeting encounter—who has never been acknowledged legally by his father, is in his twenties when he has to deliver a telegram to the father of thirteen-year-old Fermina Daza. Florentino delivers the telegram and then sees through the window two women, the younger reading to the older. Fermina lifts her head briefly to see who is walking by: "And that casual glance," García Márquez writes, "was the beginning of a cataclysm of love that still had not ended half a century later" (1989, 55).

They fall in love, but unbridgeable sociocultural differences prevent them from marrying. Fermina marries someone from her own social class and remains faithful to him for fifty years. She never says whether they loved each other. García Márquez writes, "Neither he [her husband] nor she could have said if their mutual dependence was based on love or convenience, but they had never asked the question with their hands on their hearts because both had always preferred not to know the answer" (26). In the fifty years that Fermina is married, Florentino has exactly 622 affairs.

Fermina's husband, Dr. Urbino, dies as a result of a fall from a mango tree where he is trying to catch his pet parrot, which has been insulting him for hours from the tree.

> No one realized in time that [the parrot's] wings were too
> long, and they were about to clip them that morning when
> he escaped to the top of the mango tree. And for three hours
> they had not been able to catch him. The servant girls, with the
> help of other maids in the neighborhood, had used all kinds
> of tricks to lure him down, but he insisted on staying where
> he was, laughing madly as he shouted, "Long live the Liberal
> Party, long live the Liberal Party." (24)

Finally, at a complete loss, Dr. Urbino climbs the tree himself. The higher he climbs, the higher the parrot climbs. He finally manages to catch the parrot around the neck.

> But he released him immediately because the ladder slipped
> from under his feet, and for an instant he was suspended in air,
> and then he realized that he had died without Communion,
> without time to repent of anything or to say goodbye to any-
> one, at seven minutes after four on Pentecost Sunday. (42)

Following Fermina's husband's funeral, Florentino declares his love again. "'Fermina,' he said, 'I have waited for this opportunity for more than half a century, to repeat to you once again my vow of eternal fidelity and everlasting love'" (50). He is thrown out of the house, but when Fermina wakes up the next day, she realizes that while sobbing in her sleep, she thought more about Florentino than about her husband (52).

A deep correspondence ensues and finally, after more than half a century, Florentino, who has in the meantime become president of a shipping company, invites Fermina to take a trip on one of his boats. On the *New Fidelity (La Nueva Fidelidad)*, a kind of Mississippi steamboat, they travel to a new destiny. But even though they are together on a boat, there is still no intimacy, no lasting relationship. To achieve that, Florentino comes up with a trick: the idea of cholera. Upon arrival at their destined port, he tells the captain to ask all of the passengers to disembark. The yellow flag is raised—a sign that cholera is on board ("The only thing that would allow them to bypass all that was a case of cholera on board" [342])—and Florentino has the captain set course for the port from which they sailed. When they reach that port, the captain asks desperately what he should do:

> [Without blinking] . . . [Florentino] said: "Let us keep going,
> going, going, back to La Dorada." . . .
> "And how long do you think we can keep up this goddamn
> coming and going?" [the captain] asked.

> Florentino Ariza had kept his answer ready for fifty-three
> years, seven months, and eleven days and nights.
> "Forever," he said. (348)

What do we see if we read the book as a metaphor for intercultural communication? Fermina represents the monoculture—a culture imprisoned by its own rules. Only what happens in one's own culture is good and acceptable. Not only does she obey these rules, but she also is their victim: she once fell in love with an outsider. The principle of eccentricity—i.e., that a human being is more than the culture or the morality he or she practices—is not respected. There is little willingness to interact with others, to learn from others, to make oneself vulnerable. Nonetheless, it is possible to love the other. How? We still have to explore that.

Florentino's life represents the multicultural pitfall, the multicultural fallacy, *boutique multiculturalisme*.[1] Everything is permitted, as long as it is different. That which is different is accepted as long as the differences are not deep and do not obligate one to change one's way of life and perception of reality. People are thrilled by differences. They see only the many colors of the flower, while the weeds that grow rank at the roots remain hidden to them. Of the 622 affairs Florentino had over the fifty years—none was satisfying, none was stable, none was nourished by actual concentration. The contacts were momentary, the conversations were fleeting, and the interest in each other was superficial.

But how then is the relationship between these two old people—between these radically differing cultural patterns—turned into a love story? How does Fermina escape the loneliness and stagnation of the monoculture and Florentino the limitless transience of multicultural longing? The secret is the boat, the *New Fidelity*; the captain (Samaritano in the story); and cholera. These are the conditions.

The boat is the Third Bank of the River—not your bank, not mine, but a bank in between, as anthropologists like to say. The boat sails back and forth—*toda una vida*—under the flag of cholera: Fermina and Florentino are condemned to each other and also want to be. "My God . . . ships make me so crazy,"[2] Fermina says, looking back on the completely insane turn her future and life have taken and indicating that ships—this third place—can do strange things with people (335).

In addition to the place, we find a number of things that, according to García Márquez, are fundamental for a love that transcends boundaries. The masks must fall away: the new intimacy demands that the old bodies disrobe in front of each other. They do do that, with the lights on.[3] The past experiences of living and suffering are not erased or wished away but placed within the perspective of new

1. For definitions of the positive and negative uses of the term, see, e.g., Huggan (2001, 124ff.).
2. "¡Dios mío—dijo—que loca soy en los buques!" (García Márquez 1985, 456)
3. "Pero volvió el mismo día, a la hora insólita de las once de la mañana, fresco y restaurado, y se desnudó frente a ella con una cierta ostentación. Ella se complació en verlo a plena luz tal como lo había imaginado en la oscuridad: un hombre sin edad, de piel oscura, lúcida y tensa como un paraguas abierto . . ." (1985, 463).

love: "She began to speak of her dead husband in the present tense, as if he were alive" (García Márquez 1989, 329).Then there are the letters Florentino writes to Fermina after her husband dies, expressing thoughts of such beauty and clarity that they guide her through the mourning process. She feels as if the letters are inspired by the Holy Spirit itself. The letters do not speak of domination, of power, of taking into possession or of conquering; rather, they speak of what sharing life, love, and death could mean to people, to them. They show her love as a state of grace.

And there are also the small things: he dresses up for her, and she notices it! She cries, and he sees her tears. The endless vulnerability of both: "I smell like an old woman," she says (329), and he smells it. When he walks away, he remembers that he himself smells like an old man and that she must have smelled him with the same emotion that he had felt in smelling her.

But perhaps the most important element in the story is this: cultural studies speak of the willingness to interact with others. In García Márquez's story, this is shown in a small gesture of love. In a dark cabin on the ship, Fermina and Florentino are together for the first time. It has to happen now—she is in her seventies and he in his eighties! He is extremely nervous and breaks out into a cold sweat. How do I begin? How do I approach this? One of the most beautiful scenes from the book follows: "Then he reached out with two icy fingers in the darkness, felt for the other hand in the darkness, and found it waiting for him. Both were lucid enough to realize, at the same fleeting instant, that the hands made of old bones were not the hands they had imagined before touching" (329).

Reality and imagination make a covenant with love. We will leave our interpretation of *Love in the Time of Cholera* at this.

A New Field of Research

Empirical Hermeneutics, Interculturality, and Holy Scripture is the first in a new series of monographs initiated by the Foundation Dom Hélder Câmara Chair, VU University Amsterdam. The focus of this series—intercultural hermeneutics—is very much in line with the ideas and passions of Dom Hélder Câmara (1909–1999).

Câmara—bishop of the poor, bishop of peace—was the archbishop of one of the poorest regions of Brazil, Olinda and Recife in the northeast. He and Pele were the most famous Brazilians in the world in the 1960s and 70s. This was the heyday of the Second Vatican

Dom Hélder Câmara

Council, and then of liberation theology. It was also the heyday of many military dictatorships in Latin America.

Looking back on the life of Câmara, the question arises, who in the churches actually resisted in these dark times of disappearances and torture? Câmara was one of those. His famous statement, "If I give the poor food, they call me a saint; if I ask why the poor have no food, they call me a communist," indicates where he stood. He was called the red bishop. His resistance was never bitter; he hated the violence of weapons. His weapons were texts from the Christian tradition, hope, and a great deal of humor.

While not an academic, Câmara provided impulses for research. The board of trustees of Dom Hélder Câmara Chair has created space in which new, relevant, and topical research can be done.[4] Many of Câmara's visions have been fulfilled: small groups—the Abrahamic minorities, if you will; the dialogue on the sacred texts; the perspective of liberation, justice, and peace; the permanent interaction between North and South,[5] and the small gesture of love: the hand that lies ready for those who seek him.

This space is that of empirical hermeneutics in intercultural perspective. In short, it has to do with the question of whether reading Bible stories jointly by groups from often radically different cultural and sociopolitical contexts can contribute to transformation and changed perspectives. In which ways can an intercultural dialogue on the meaning of fundamental narratives—Holy Scripture—contribute to justice and liberation? Can cultural differences, when rendered hermeneutically operative, not give such depth to the dialogue on the meaning of these stories that faith becomes what it is ultimately meant to be, a searching and reaching for the truth?

The chair has a twofold focus. Shape is given to a new practice on the one hand, and there is reflection on the formulation of theory on the other. The new practice consists of bringing small groups together, on all continents, who read the same Bible story at the same time and discuss the meaning of the story with each other. Groups of *desplazados* in Colombia read with groups of Christians from Indonesia, groups of *dalits* from India with Cuban groups, Korean students with

---

4. In the early years after its establishment, the following visiting scholars held the Dom Hélder Câmara chair, lecturing and organizing guest lectures for students: Julio de Santa Ana (Brazil), Bas Wielenga (India), Kamal Hossain (Bangladesh), Mercy Amba Oduyoye (Ghana), Tarek Mitri (Lebanon), Daniel Schipani (Argentina/USA), Anna May Say Pa (Myanmar/Burma). Currently the focus of the person who holds this appointment is to offer courses and do research in the area of empirical cultural and interreligious hermeneutics, in particular into the question of how the process of attributing meaning to religious texts is given shape in situations of exclusion, injustice, and oppression, and of how the intercultural and interreligious discussion on the meaning of these texts can be conducted in the perspective of justice and liberation.

5. "The moral force of Action for Justice and Peace will be born of communication between the Abrahamic minorities from different towns, different countries, different continents. When the Abrahamic minorities of the Third World feel themselves truly in solidarity and, above all, when they meet fraternal echoes coming to them from the developed countries, humanity will have taken a step towards peace. The Spirit breathes where it will. It is perfectly possible for Abrahamic minorities to emerge in North and South, East and West" (Câmara 1971, 75).

Nicaraguan Pentecostals, and Dutch groups with Ghanaian or Filipino groups. But groups can also read with each other within the same region or country. Thus, reading groups of Arabic or Ghanaian Christians in the Netherlands can also be connected with groups from Dutch mainline churches.

The basic material of the formulation of theory is the reading experiences of these groups. While Holy Scripture—not only the Qur'an!—is at this time often associated with terror and destruction, and while it is often suggested that a one-to-one relationship exists between sacred texts and human actions, we actually know almost nothing about that relationship.

However, on the basis of the experiences that we have already had and about which I will share shortly, there is reason to test the hypothesis that the intercultural reading of narratives from sacred texts—in our case, the Bible—can have a beneficial effect and help readers to have more understanding for one another, leading to reconciliation and more justice. Herewith I have formulated the central question of the field of research: Can the Bible also be a positive factor in processes of development and reconciliation? Can Bible stories also be places for transformation and repentance? Can Bible stories also be places for conversations on peace—even when they are what Phyllis Trible called "texts of terror" (Trible 1984)?

1

The Field of Research

I will now describe the challenges of this field of research in a few steps, defining several essential terms and discussing and reflecting on examples from practice.

The Challenge

I will call the challenge that we want to take up "the remarkable paradox of Holy Scripture." This paradox can be described as follows. In every discipline that is concerned with the understanding of texts, it is assumed that reading also has a consequence, a moment of appropriation, an effect. Sociolinguists speak of texts and narratives as bearers of potential behavior: "A text . . . does not have a single, closed meaning, but a 'meaning potential,' or more appropriately in a functional framework, 'behaviour potential.' The text, from this point of view, is a range of possibilities, an open-ended set of options in behaviour that are available to the individual interpreter" (Blount 1995, 17).

The Turn to the Reader

Since the last decades of the twentieth century, the discovery of the importance of the reader in processes of interpretation has translated into a true "turn to the reader." In almost all disciplines having to do with language and texts, there has been a new orientation since the 1970s, one that is reader centered rather than text centered.[1]

---

1. One can think here of speech act theories or of the research into the performative character of language (a death sentence, test results from the doctor). In the reader response theories coming out of literary studies, some go so far as to see the reader as the co-author of the text. Interpretive communities, with their own conventions and interests, are determinative for interpretation, according to Stanley Fish (1980). There is nothing like a "correct" reading process. Interpretation is the source of texts, facts, authors, and intentions; everything is the result of interpretation. In his well-known book *The Double Perspective,* David Bleich (1988) makes a vehement argument for more interaction between professional readers in the academy and ordinary readers. The perspective is theoretical and North American and does not cover the interaction, for example, between rich and poor or between Western and non-Western readers. Ideological critique, as formulated by Althusser (1972) and Eagleton (1976), also

Objections

Two fundamental objections to these developments were expressed at the time. The first objection was that people spoke endlessly about the reader but actually engaged the reader very little in conversation, and little empirical research was done. The implied reader, the model reader, the ideal reader, and the ideal reading community often were mentioned, but much of this was done on an abstract level—referring to reading strategies in general, reading communities in general, and general relationships between texts and readers.[2]

The second objection was that proper reading was very normatively formulated by hermeneuticians, philosophers, and linguists, and that much was demanded of the ideal—often Western and well-educated—readers.[3] To be able to read, people had to know and be able to do so much that it was asked, "But what do (ordinary) readers themselves do with texts?"

---

is concerned with the reader. Every reader approaches a text with expectations and interests. The engagement with the text is almost always conflictual: expectations are not met, tension arises, and a rift occurs. Ideological critique wants to trace this interaction. How is it explained? How is it modified? How is it eliminated? What criteria guide the process? Why is this element of the text privileged and that one silenced? But it also holds true that ideological critique was developed abstractly and was seldom in dialogue with ordinary readers.

2. The lack of empirical research within biblical studies led Hans Robert Jauss, Hans-Georg Gadamer's student, to sigh as late as 1982, "In biblical studies (one) has not yet begun to attend seriously to the reception history of biblical texts. As long as biblical reader-response critics concentrate on the implied reader and narratee in the biblical texts, they will continue to neglect the reception of biblical texts by flesh-and-blood readers" (Jauss 1982). Jauss himself, with his aesthetic reception, focused attention on the reader's horizon of expectation. Each reader brings a certain perspective to the text. This point of view is loaded with a reference framework, experiences, and expectations. Jauss is moving cautiously toward the new field of an empirical hermeneutics. He develops a model for the analysis of identification patterns between readers and characters in a story (association, admiration, and sympathy) but does not come any further than an analysis of motivation for the identification (Jauss 1982).

3. The reader must respond to the invitation of the text, follow the reading strategies of the text (Eco), be able to enjoy the pleasure of the text (Barthes), be capable of an aesthetic response (*ästhetische Wirkung*; Iser), be open to the transforming effect of reading the Bible (Thiselton), be able to formulate an interpretative hypothesis (Hirsch), be sensitive to the affective semantics of the text, i.e., be open to the power of the text to move (rhetorical criticism), be able to discover the ideological seizures of power that hide behind every text (ideological criticism), be able to connect with each other both intertextual (connecting of other texts with the one concerned) and extratextual relations (application of the text or connecting the meaning of the text to historical events) of a text (Pierce, communicative analysis). And we have still not addressed the question of how the reader should see the status of the text and which attitude he should take vis-à-vis the text: one of trust, one of suspicion, one of declaring the text invalid (annihilation; some black, feminist, and postcolonial hermeneutics). Should the reading process be directed at retrieval, survival (liberation theologies), or resistance (Tracy)? The reading of the text should be connected with a (liberation) praxis (emancipation hermeneutics); the interpretation of the text should be in service to an analysis of the context (Tracy); the "knowing understanding," in which the moment of appropriation occurs, has become acquainted with the results of exegesis (Ricoeur), etc.

The Turn to the Empirical Reader

The turn to the empirical reader truly began in the West[4] only a few decades ago.[5] We still often encounter statistical and quantitative research that is directed at people's reading behavior—how much do they read, when, and why. Such research can deal with the question of the rise of a literary canon (for example, in schools), and of which social interactions and actors (schools, teachers, politics, publishers, prize systems, etc.) in the cultural field (Bourdieu) preserve this canon. How do literary taste and preference arise? Why do people buy the books they buy, and who buys them? Why is it so difficult for women to be accepted into a literary canon (Vogel 2001)? What is foundational for the empirical sociology of literature is the explanation of an interpretation of a text by a reader and the attention to the institutions surrounding it: the writer's reputation, the reader's behavior, the mechanisms that attribute quality. While we try to make use of these insights, this research is not always our concern. A theologian, biblical scholar, or hermeneutician who wants to investigate what happens when a group of Colombian *desplazados* reads the same biblical text as a Dutch group is dependent on a unique analytical tool.[6]

The Reader in Religious Traditions

Regardless of the above, all hermeneutical traditions of all religions based on sacred texts argue *a fortiori* that texts do something with their readers. All theologians know that if the text is cut off from a current, living community, it is reduced to a cadaver on which an autopsy is performed (Ricoeur 1998, xii). Reception, a response from the readers, is constitutive for the meaning of texts, for the meaning of tradition, and indeed, for the meaning of revelation itself.

In the reception history of Bible texts there has always been reflection on the relationship between text and reception, directed for the most part at the relationship between the status of the text and the freedom of the reader. The whole Christian tradition sees the importance of reading as a response to the written text, but the relationship is not always understood in the same way (de Wit 2008). That which is viewed as self evident gives way to wrestling. Both partners are seen as going separate ways, and attempts are made to restore the situation to health. A brief overview can clarify the task that confronts us.

Story as Torah

In the Old Testament tradition, the relationship between the text and the living community is beautifully expressed. Here reception is not simply reading the text; rather, it is a new word that is stated about and on the basis of the text: the writ-

---

4. In disciplines like the sociology of literature, empirical sociology of literature, empirical reception theory, reception aesthetics, and empirical literary studies, but also cognitive psychology and experimental psychology.

5. In France, the first reader survey occurred in 1955, according to Joëlle Bahloul (1998/2002).

6. In her study on reading behavior among so-called *lecteurs faibles* in France, Joëlle Bahloul expresses critique of the established sociology of literature in France. What is important is not how much someone reads but the way reading is capitalized on in the social, emotional, and active life of a reader.

ten Torah has the oral Torah as its partner for life. There is no division between the two. The second Torah—the oral one—is an expansion of the first, a sign of its vitality and ability to fill the horizon anew (Ricoeur 1998, xii).

The Patristics

In patristic hermeneutics there is a close relationship between text and response by later readers. The threefold and later fourfold meaning of Scripture in the Patristics can be seen primarily as a way of saying that Bible texts also have—in addition to a context-bound, historical meaning—an ethical and spiritual potential that is intended to be operationalized.[7]

The Reformation

However much the Reformers emphasized the importance of the *sensus literalis* and were allergic to floating allegories, and however much the dominant historical-critical research emerged from the Reformation period with a phobia about what nonprofessional readers would do with Bible texts, this does not mean that reception was not important. Rather, it means that there was an allergy to a certain kind of reception. Indeed, one can say that it is precisely the emphasis on the *sensus literalis* that expresses the longing for Bible texts to be appropriated in a historical and sociopolitical way.

Calvin adheres very much to the principle reformulated later by Gadamer that "application" is an essential part of the interpretation process—not merely an extra or third phase. Hans Frei, in his well-known book *The Eclipse of Biblical Narrative*, cites with approval Hans Joachim Kraus's statement that, for Calvin, the Bible is not so much inspired but "communicates and informs" as its main purpose. There is no doubt that Calvin was thinking not only of the original hearers of the Bible texts but primarily of himself and his contemporaries.[8] What happened with the Bible in Strasbourg, Geneva, Germany, the Netherlands, and wherever else during the time of the Reformation, has everything to do with reception, with a response, with *relectura* in the sense of double transformation: a new reading by a new reader renews the meaning of the text. The rise of what Gerben Heitink calls a "biblical consciousness" (2001, 59) is primarily a response by readers to a way of living with Bible texts.[9]

---

7. The classic adage from the thirteenth century was *Littera gesta docet / quid credas allegoria / moralis quid agat / quo tendas anagogia*: praxis, faith, ethics, and eschatology.

8. Frei writes, quoting Kraus approvingly: "The Bible is, for Calvin, not inspired and hence does not itself in the first place inspire, but communicates and informs" (1974, 21).

9. It is peculiar to see how all kinds of Reformation views of Scripture have received new life in the recent lay movements centered on the Bible in Latin America and now in Africa. In his book *Ordinary Bible Reading*, Mark Labberton describes the use of the Bible in the Strasbourg of the Reformation in a way that very much reminds one of Bible movements such as the one taking shape at this time in the Two-Thirds World (sometimes also designated as Third World). The communal, communitarian reading of the Bible must be seen as a theological idea of the Reformation, Labberton writes. He shows how the percentage of literate people rose enormously in Strasbourg after 1540. There was a new interaction between the biblical text and ordinary readers (Labberton 1990, 290ff.).

The Enlightenment

Indeed, something went very wrong in the Enlightenment between Brother Text and Sister Appropriation. The problems in the relationship began to become visible in the late Renaissance, and the divorce occurred in the Enlightenment (de Wit 2008). Reason and (primarily Western) logic became the arbiters of meaning (Ricoeur), viewing the diverse, exotic, arbitrary, bizarre, and often narcissistic appropriation processes as problematic. In the Enlightenment, the contextual pole of the process of understanding—the response to the text—was seen as suspect and superficial. Exegesis went its own way, historically oriented, often arrogantly—convinced that Bible texts were stable objects and that exploring the historical context exhausted the meaning potential of the texts. The exegete became a *Vormund,* a guardian.

However varied the development of Western biblical studies was, "Lady Appropriation" was increasingly ignored—viewed as irrelevant, as a hindrance, and indeed as an assault on the original meaning of the text. It was not until the middle of the twentieth century that the objections raised by the fields of literary studies (fallacy of origins), modern hermeneutics (all understanding is contextual), and postmodern philosophy (dissemination, intertextuality, connection between interpretation and power) gained a foothold and the limitations and one-sidedness of the Enlightenment paradigm began to be seen. The price was high and the way back difficult.

Genitive Theologies

The way back—the rehabilitation of Lady Appropriation as an elementary component in the process of attributing meaning—has been traveled in recent years more intensively in the non-Western context than anywhere else. Those who know about the Bible movement in Latin America (de Wit 1991), Africa (Ukpong 2000; West 1997, 1999, 2000; Dube 2001; West and Dube 1996), and Asia, and have seen the results, will be deeply impressed by the opportunities that dialogue between exegetes and ordinary, socioeconomically poor readers offers. For many exegetes working on these continents, the relationship between text and the response to it is precious. It is a relationship fundamental to the hermeneutics of liberation. Reading the Bible in communities is good for people and helps change the world. But, in however nuanced a way Latin American biblical scholars such as José Severino Croatto, Carlos Mesters, Milton Schwantes, Pablo Richard, and many others talk about this connection between reading and the praxis of liberation, one hears too often about a longing—the hoped-for effect of reading the Bible for a praxis of liberation. Moreover, the relationship is formulated in an almost causal way, as if everyone in Latin America read the Bible[10] and as if this would automatically lead all readers to a praxis of liberation in the sociopolitical meaning of the word.[11]

---

10. A recent statistical study in Chile pointed out that among the Roman Catholics (65.5 percent of the population) 53 percent say that they never or almost never read the Bible. See Aldunate 2008, 22.

11. "Reading with" has just begun in Africa (end of the 1990s) and has produced intense debates on who the ordinary African reader is and what a genuine African hermeneutics is. See Adamo 1999.

Does the new praxis—reading the Bible "with" the people—not take the bite out of our paradox? Has the challenge we are addressing here not already been taken up? My answer is no—to the contrary! However fascinating the stories may be about how "the people, the poor" read the Bible, not even a beginning has been made in Latin America—as far as I can see—with respect to a systematic analysis of the empirical material that the people have produced in abundance.[12] Rather, it must be said that precisely the lack of empirical research leads to all kinds of romantic and essentialist statements about how the Bible is read among the poor. Sometimes, descriptions of the relationship between people and the Bible correspond more to the desires of the socially engaged exegete than to the reality. And here as well, there are all kinds of demands that readers, good readers, must meet. In other words, a look at the Latin American and African situations accentuates precisely our paradox and makes the challenge all the more urgent: if it is claimed that Bible reading is good for people and contributes to liberation, let us see how that works.

Two Remarks

The relationship between reading and praxis is more complex than many—on both the left and the right—often want to have us believe. Allow me to make two remarks on the complexity of this relationship.

The first is an example. In a study conducted in the United States in 2007, people were asked about their view of six miracle stories in the Bible—Jesus' resurrection, Daniel in the lions' den, creation happening in six days, the Israelites' crossing of the Red Sea, Jesus walking on water, and the story of David and Goliath. According to the study, the data indicated that "the typical American has adopted these accounts as the foundation of a valued faith in God." At least 75 percent of all of those interviewed said that they believe in the literal meaning of the resurrection story; whether they thought the other stories had also happened literally or not depended very much on their politics, ethnic background, and church affiliation. The study's final conclusion is instructive: For a great majority of those interviewed, it appeared that belief in the literal meaning of these stories did not play any role in their lives, however foundational they understood these stories to be. This led the researchers to make the following statement:

> In fact, a minority of the people who believe these stories to be
> true consistently apply the principles embedded in these stories
> within their own lives. It seems that millions of Americans
> believe the Bible content is true but are not willing to translate
> those stories into action. Sadly, for many people, the Bible has
> become a respected but impersonal religious history lesson that
> stays removed from their life.[13]

---

12. In Spanish-speaking countries, including most countries in Latin America, hardly any research has been done into the reading practices of readers, according to Goldin in the foreword to Bahloul; on this see Bahloul 2002, 1–3.
13 A recent American study among Bible readers was presented under the heading: "Most Americans Take

The second remark concerns an issue that plays a role in all religions of the Book—namely, the difference between the attentive and careful reading of texts and the use of those texts. The complexity of the relationship between reading and praxis becomes somewhat clearer when we discover the importance of this relationship.[14] Holy Scripture invokes many reactions, but not all of them have to do with reading. Reading is not the same as using. All religious traditions have what Umberto Eco has called "gastronomic reading."[15] This does not have much to do with reading anymore, but with the use of the book to which the texts refer.[16] This

---

Well-Known Bible Stories at Face Value." The results of the study are surprising: six "well-known Bible stories are accepted as literal truth by an average of two out of three adults." But for those who love the Bible and will be cheered by these results, the final conclusion of the study is also surprising: "But Barna [the one conducting the study] also noted a significant disconnection between faith and practice. 'While the level of literal acceptance of these Bible stories is nothing short of astonishing given our cultural context, the widespread embrace of these accounts raises questions about the unmistakable gap between belief and behavior. On the one hand we have tens of millions of people who view these narratives as reflections of the reality, the authority and the involvement of God in our lives. On the other hand, a majority of those same people harbor a stubborn indifference toward God and His desire to have intimacy with them. In fact, a minority of the people who believe these stories to be true consistently apply the principles embedded in these stories within their own lives. It seems that millions of Americans believe the Bible content is true, but are not willing to translate those stories into action. Sadly, for many people, the Bible has become a respected but impersonal religious history lesson that stays removed from their life.'"

This report is based upon a nationwide telephone survey conducted by The Barna Group in August 2007 among a random sample of 1000 adults, age 18 and older. For further details see: http://www.barna.org /barna-update/article/18-congregations/92-most-americans-take-well-known-bible-stories-at-face-value (Oct. 21, 2007). In this context one should also consult the study by Hijme Stoffels of possession of the Bible and Bible usage in the Netherlands.

14. Edwin Koster refers in his dissertation to the importance of Umberto Eco's distinction (in: Eco, *Kant e l'ornitorinco*) between reading/interpretation and the use of texts (Koster 2005, 225ff. and elsewhere). The use of a text—action as result of a reading process—is not the same as a rhetorical reading, which refers to the way texts persuade or convince readers by means of their argumentative structure.

15. See Eco 1997, 107ff. With this term Eco has in mind non-critical, consumptive reading. One does not allow oneself to be carried along by the text; there is no interaction; the text is consumed.

16. For this see the examples of the use of the psalms that Adamo gives in his essay on African hermeneutics (1999): "We should use Psalm 109 to resist strongly the power of our enemies. According to Chief Ogunfuye's rule, we should go into the field in the middle of the night and light three candles—one to the North, one to the East, one to the West. We ourselves should stand in the middle and read this psalm with the name of God (El), the name of the enemy and our own name in mind. If we are suffering from a swollen stomach, we should pray one of the therapeutic psalms, Psalms 1, 2, 3, 20, or 40. Then we draw fresh water from the river, pour it into a new pot, cut up palm leaves in it, say the name Eli Safatan 62 times and light nine candles. We should bathe in this water for nine days. If we cannot, then we should recite these psalms with our head in a pot containing a mixture of fried oil, coconut oil and cow urine. That will get rid of our our backache, toothache or headache. If our spouse is barren, we should ask her to drink a mixture of coconut milk and raw eggs; then she is to read Psalm 51, naked on the field, early in the morning after we have slept with her. Finally, if we had to write an exam, we should pray one of the success psalms. We should write the name of our school on a piece of parchment, burn it, mix it with water, drink that and then recite Psalm 8."

Whoever thinks that this African way of using the psalms, associated immediately with wholeness and healing, is unique should look at how the psalms have been used in Kabbalistic circles since the seventeenth century. The words, the letters, the vocalization, the accents—everything in the psalms was used to ask for known and unknown favors. They were used for a long life, for forgiveness, infertility, health,

use often occurs without any hermeneutical mediation—without the text being given the chance to do something with the reader—simply because of the status of the book. One can think here of the Book as a cultural legacy, as a product, as a fetish; one can think of the use of the ink, the paper, the cover, the pictures; the Book as book, the magic, its status, the Book as amulet; and the use of the Book for healing, health, success, enchantment, war, domination, swearing an oath, repentance, prosperity, fertility, and so on and so forth. The well-known "thumb method" of reading is a good example of this phenomenon: asking a question, placing one's thumb on an arbitrary place in the Bible and, *voilà*—an answer.

Both remarks emphasize again the well-known insight that what people do with sacred texts is more than a product of an intrinsic quality of the Sacred Book itself; it is possible to use the book in ways that are informed by many kinds of nonreligious influences that primarily have to do with social inequality and power.

The Challenge Again

In the meantime, the challenge that we want to take up has been articulated sufficiently. What has happened in literary studies in recent decades has not happened in theology: research into the insight held everywhere that texts do something with readers, and readers do something with texts. But what is being investigated as a premise in literary studies is—in Christian theology—not only a longing, a hoped-for result. It is a demand, a condition for survival. Without readers, without a response, the Scripture ceases to be a source of revelation. Empirical research in this area is urgent.

Any attempt to survey this field of research—empirical research into the reception of Bible texts—will lead to dizziness. Great modesty is the only solution here.[17] But we have an advantage, in terms of quantity, over empirical literary studies that research published books. The number of published titles is increasing spectacularly: in Dutch-speaking areas alone, there were 3,000 new titles around the year 1900, and 20,000 new titles around the year 2000. In the US, 85,000 new titles appeared in 1947, and 1.3 million in 1998. In our field of investigation, however, we are studying one book, the most-sold book in the history of humanity. And there is still something else that makes this field of research spe-

---

hostile governments, business, etc. Psalm snippets, single verses, or even parts of them were taken completely out of their literary and historical context in the Jewish liturgies—very early on already—throughout the centuries until now, playing a role in the liturgy and constituting, as it were, a genuine part of a script for a sacred drama (Attridge and Fassler 2003, 33ff.). Such psalm snippets are found everywhere in the world. There is no taxi or bus in Latin America where Psalm 23 does not hang on the rearview mirror: "El señor es mi pastor." The psalms were undoubtedly used in such a way in Israel as well.

17. See also the remark by Bert Vanheste (1981, 193): "The influence that goes out from literature comes into being in the encounter between the literary work and the reader. Unfortunately . . . [this] field of research, the reading public, is still in a beginning phase of exploration. Moreover, it is to be feared that even the most advanced exploratory techniques will largely fail because the ground is too swampy. The researcher into the effect of literature on the reader has no firm ground to stand on. The swamp is uncommonly rich in compositon, but no one can get a grip on it. After all, literature does not have influence in isolation."

cial. Apart from all of the special characteristics of the Bible as text, it is a fact that no single other book is being read at the same time by so many different people in such radically different contexts and situations. The discovery of the hermeneutical dimension of that fact and the possibilities that it offers for intercultural communication are staggering.

Before we move on to the Bible readers in Africa and the Andes, I must first make good on a promise to define a number of terms. Empirical hermeneutics— directed at the reading of Bible texts—in an intercultural setting? That demands definition and clarity.

2

Empirical Hermeneutics in Intercultural Perspective

Hermeneutics refers to the theoretical practice that reflects on the question of how interpretation processes of texts occur. Hermeneutics is not the interpretation itself—for that one can better use the concept *hermeneuse*—but the academic reflection on how the processes work. What instruments and factors play a role? Where do the differences come from? Who are the players in the field, and what are their roles? In the case of hermeneutics of the Bible, we are concerned with the interpretation of biblical texts. The use of the term "interpretation process" is intended to indicate that more is at stake in reading and understanding the Bible than simply an academic interpretation. There is no reason why hermeneutics should not look at the processes involved in interpreting texts locally. Exegesis—when directed at the question of what Bible texts could have meant in their historical setting—is one phase in a more comprehensive process, in which interpreting the text in the local context and the praxes of contemporary readers play a role.

The Descriptive Dimension

The addition of the adjective *empirical* refers to the target group and to the descriptive dimension of this hermeneutics. It means that we are attempting to map—or at least define—the contours of how flesh-and-blood readers deal with texts. It thus concerns a form of reception criticism, no longer directed solely at the great men in the tradition (as was customary until recently), but concerning the question of how contemporary readers—primarily ordinary readers—work with texts. Empirical hermeneutics thus includes an analysis of the appropriation processes and is directed at the text in its relationship to local explanation and interpretation, and in its effect on and use by contemporary readers. Empirical hermeneutics seeks to explore the area where the behavior potential of the text becomes operational.

Sociologists often begin to tremble when a theologian uses the term *empirical*. That is unnecessary; there is no reason (apart from some extra training, which can't do any harm) why an empirical method like Grounded Theory—with its back-and-forth movement between the content of the empirical material and its own hypotheses (Glaser and Strauss 1967; Glaser 1993)—cannot be made fruitful hermeneutically and applied within biblical hermeneutics. Biblical hermeneutics has the capacity to explore this area with sensitivity and care and to develop an adequate code system to study the reception of Bible stories on a meta-level.[1] The empirical material—reading reports—can be divided into text segments, semantic units to which labels and codes can be attached.[2] Balance and care can be exercised in weighing what people are finding against what the empirical material offers. The empirical material can correct and enrich the hypotheses as, in the analysis of each reading, report codes are added until a saturation point is reached.

Simple data can thus be mapped in a number of main categories. A first such category can include the socioeconomic and ethnic background of the readers, composition of the group, church affiliation, how the readers see their relationship to society, age, context, motivation,[3] group dynamic aspects of the interpretation process and the cultural determination of those (e.g., are there traces of a collectivist culture or an oral culture?), the liturgical form of the meeting, the group dynamic, etc.

In a second main category, the more exegetical-hermeneutical aspects of the interpretation process can be coded: the reading attitude (open, questioning,

---

1. For an extensive description of the way in which empirical material is coded, see de Wit 2004, 395–436.
2. De Wit 2004a, 400: "The first phase of this type of qualitative analysis reduces the overwhelming amount of text data by identifying the content of more or less encompassing text segments. Then, a code—abbreviation or name—is attached to this text segment. In what follows, these codes are used to represent text segments or units of meaning in the text. Fundamentally, this is a process of categorization, where the categories may emerge during text interpretation or may be taken from an already existing category system, depending on the researcher's epistemological orientation. During the second phase, researchers try to reconstruct the text producer's subjective meaning system from the units of meaning in their text data. In the third and final phase, researchers try to infer invariants or general commonalities by comparing individual systems of meaning."
3. Why have groups participated in the project, and what does this imply for the course of the interaction with the partner group? What reasons led the group to participate? A distinction can be made between affective and cognitive motivation. Affective motivation leads groups to participate because they want to help, want to make a better world, decrease asymmetry, etc. Much research has been done on the coherence between cognitive motivation and possibilities for changing beliefs—for example, in interactions between Palestinian and Jewish groups. "When a set of beliefs of one group is incompatible with a set of beliefs of the other group, this situation is defined as cognitive discrepancy"; "In a conflict situation, the cognitive discrepancy involves incompatibility of beliefs regarding solutions, incompatibility in the accounts of the background or the course of the conflict, and other contents" (Bar-Tal 1990). A certain sort of motivation leads to the freezing of (faith) insights that are based on knowledge, and another kind of motivation leads to thawing. The factors can be analyzed that lead to hardening (freezing) or softening (thawing) major differences in insights and convictions, in epistemic or cognitive discrepancy. A distinction is made between motivation for validity (1), motivation for structure (2), and motivation for specific content (3). The motivation for validity leads the most to growth from discrepancy to consensus. The motivation for specific content leads the most to the freezing of convictions or faith insights (beliefs) that are based on knowledge. See Bar Tal 1990.

academic, problematizing the text, dogmatic, pietistic, psychologizing, liberation-focused, etc.—including the cultural determination of the reading attitude and the heuristic keys used); the status of the text for the readers; and the strategies for explaining the text. When using aids such as commentaries, do people look primarily at the historical background of the text, at the text as text (as a literary, narrative, and rhetorical unit), at the foreground of the text, at the text in its wider literary context, or at inter- and intratextuality? On what verses do people concentrate, and why? How do people fill in the narrative gaps of the text? How do they perceive the actants in the text—with which of them do they identify, and why? What do they consider to be the central message of the text? Which translation do they use, and why, and what is the effect of this translation on the interpretation of the text? We could go on.

A third main category can concentrate on the element of appropriation and application. If the text is applied to the local context (i.e., fused with the reader's own life story), is the text's original reference replaced by a contemporary one? If so, how? What strategy is used: an allegorical model; a historical, analogical one; a tracing-paper model; a model of parallelism of terms (e.g., Pharaoh is Pinochet; we are the people of Israel); parallelism of relationships (e.g., Pharaoh is Pinochet, and we are the people of Israel, and just as Pharaoh oppressed Israel, so Pinochet oppresses us); or the *Dialog der Verhältnisse*?[4]

Subsequently, what is the content of the appropriation—eternal life, grace, reconciliation, liberation, redemption, "God's promises are fulfilled in my life," strength, etc.? What is its relationship to the readers' views—confirming, narcissistic, (self-)critical, problematizing, believing that biblical values must be overruled, etc.? Finally, what is the actual, measurable praxeological effect of the appropriation: there is no appropriation, it remains on the level of "we should . . . ," a new lifestyle, altruism, conversion, involvement in resistance movements, new forms of sociopolitical action, diaconal work, missions, evangelization, transformation in the perception of the other, etc.?

After the simple factors of the interpretation process have been thus mapped, one can search for significant correlations. These are found in the back-and-forth movement between one's own hypotheses/research questions and the empirical material itself, primarily via a comparative method; the hundreds of reading reports are compared with one another through software specially developed for qualitative research, and—on the basis of these results—significant correlations are formulated. In our case we will explore the coherence between the effect

---

4. The central question here is how, via which strategy, the text is applied locally. If by appropriation we understand the process by which the original reference of a text is replaced by a new one, then how does this process work with the reading groups? To categorize this, we use classical models from hermeneutics that are all found in the reading reports: allegorical, typological, model of the parallelism of terms (also called the tracing paper model), the correspondence of relationships model (Boff 1980), and a *Dialog der Verhältnisse* model. This last model is described by van der Ven, and he relates it critically to the correspondence of relationships model used by C. Boff. The concept of correspondence proceeds too much from agreement; there must also be room for criticism and confrontation. "The concept of dialogue offers . . . this space, for dialogue is indeed directed toward agreement but does not proceed from it" (van der Ven 1994).

of poverty and wealth on interpretation, the effect of the cultural context, the coherence between the direct sociopolitical context and the heuristic keys of the readers,[5] the effect of the dominant reading traditions—including those in the church—and their relationship to readers' willingness to interact with others,[6] and identification patterns, etc.

The Normative Dimension: Intercultural as an Ethical Concept

Hermeneutics can be directed at specific aspects of a process, at specific readers, or at specific hoped-for results of an interpretation process. One can thus investigate the issue of how reading Bible texts can serve processes of change.

Hermeneutics directed at processes of change are given a genitive label, such as Black Hermeneutics, Hermeneutics of Liberation, Feminist Hermeneutics, Dalit Hermeneutics, Calypso Hermeneutics. The label refers mainly to the interests of the subject whom the hermeneutical reflection is intended to serve: women, black people, Rastafarians, outcasts, or the poor. The list is endless. The label has a critical dimension: it refers to groups whose interests are not defended by other hermeneutics. It also has a normative dimension: people want to lay down rules for how texts must be read. The label then receives a surplus value.

Thus one sees, for example, how among Latin American, African, and Asian biblical scholars, the concept of "poor" or "black" or "outcast" is not simply a descriptive, primarily socioeconomic and ethnic concept but also a normative category. "Among us the poor have become the best interpreters of the Scripture," writes Milton Schwantes, a Brazilian (1987, 3). I have commented elsewhere on this merging of the descriptive and normative and have pointed to the trap of reduction (de Wit 1991, 2008). What I want to make clear is that if we attach the label *intercultural* to hermeneutics, we are dealing with a normative dimension; *intercultural* is not solely a way of reading the Bible that crosses geographical boundaries but is an ethically loaded concept. I will clarify what I mean through two contributions. First, I will make Hendrik Procee's reflections on cultural differences fruitful for hermeneutics; I will then use core elements from what Emmanuel Levinas says about alterity (otherness) in connection with the interpretation of texts.

Nonexclusion and Willingness to Interact

Rules for proper reading are formulated and analyzed in hermeneutical schemes. But what is proper reading? Are there a few basic rules in the multiplicity of

---

5. By *heuristic keys*, we mean the question of which elements from the reader's own context/experience are constitutive for the interpretation process as a selection process.

6. By *focalization*, we mean a variant of the theory offered by Mieke Bal: the relationship between the elements presented in the story and the view of the readers of those elements. Narrative theory, as it has developed in the course of this century, has different terms for this concept. The most usual term is *perspective* or *narrative perspective*. The following terms also occur: *narrative situations, narrative standpoints, narrative methods, point of view*, etc. But they are all unclear on one point: They do not make any distinction between the view on the basis of which the elements are presented and the identity of the body that operationalizes this view (Bal 1990, 113ff.). Primarily cultural components that also determine the interpretation process as selection process are studied under this category.

hermeneutical drafts that could apply to all drafts? Is there a normative minimum that would determine this? Thiselton has shown developments in modern hermeneutics in two directions (Thiselton 1992): a more contextual or sociopragmatic line of thinking and a more universalistic one. The same developments can be seen in cultural studies; there "universalism" and "relativism" have been of primary importance. Universalism represents a system of unity: there is one reality, one method for gaining knowledge of that reality, and one sound system of moral judgments. In all of the diversity, a coherence is sought that can serve as a guideline for human existence. In relativism, the contextual aspects and variety are central: there are many realities, many ways of gaining insight into them, and divergent systems of morality (Procee 1991).

The parallels with the developments in cultural studies are interesting for hermeneutics. In hermeneutics, one also can find universalistic schemes in contrast with those arguing for a more contextually determined approach. Formulated rather sharply, one can say that sociopragmatic or contextual hermeneutics claims that outside of context, there is nothing one can say about an interpretation of the Bible, whereas the more universalistic approach maintains that a universal framework fits each situation and is the sole source of the legitimacy of each interpretation process. Thus, Eurocentric hermeneutics have long had universal pretensions. The West also has strongly determined the demands made in literary studies and elsewhere of readers, as we have discussed already. The more relativistic and contextually determined "genitive" hermeneutics have arisen as a protest against—and evidence of—the incompleteness of Eurocentric hermeneutics.

In the current hermeneutical situation, which is sometimes described using the metaphor of a battlefield, each interpretation and approach to Scripture seems to be of as much or as little value as any other. Where can the norms be found that can produce an independent judgment? After all, both the contextual and the universalistic approaches are problematic if formulated in extremes. The contextual way nails people down to cultural values and to the social and political situation in which they happen to find themselves. Sometimes this approach results in a strong reductionism because readers merge with their context. The universalistic way gives every interpretation, every reading, the right to speak if it adheres to the universally valid frameworks that universalism itself has established. Here one often finds groups of people excluded, "strange" forms of interpretation declared inferior, and an idealism that ignores the pain of the historical moment.

How can intercultural hermeneutics offer a way out? It can do so by taking up two central concepts in cultural studies: interactive diversity and eccentricity. Interactive diversity implies the willingness to make the factor of cultural diversity operative or—in the context of this argument—visible in the way people read the Bible. For growth and exchange of perspectives to happen, confrontation is sometimes necessary. Confrontation can occur and be "organized" whenever diversity is involved in discussions of the meaning of Bible texts. But a more profound question is why interaction, an intercultural dimension, and practice can be described as qualities of the hermeneutical process. For that I have recourse to the concept of eccentricity, as used by Procee in his study on transcultural morality. The (philosophical) concept of eccentricity has to do with something specific to the structure of a human being. It refers to the insight that "the human being not only *is* a body but also *has* a body, is the master and plaything of his psyche, and product and producer of his culture." People are, and they are related to that "are." People are never completely reducible to themselves. Eccentricity leads to the multiformity of human individuals as well as to the great diversity of cultural patterns. Some cultures are strongly oriented to interaction, whereas others are concerned with stopping it. On the basis of one and the same basic structure, it is possible both to be open to new influences and to close oneself off from them. Eccentricity, as a general human characteristic, means that interactions are essential for human beings. Procee develops two norms for transcultural morality: the principle of nonexclusion and the principle of promoting interaction.[7]

The given of eccentricity also can be made fruitful for hermeneutics. People are not only products of their interpretation of the Bible; they also can acquire knowledge of other interpretations. However closed or reproductive interpretations of the Scripture are, interpreters are never completely reducible to them. Readers also can objectify their own interpretation. Thus the concept of eccentricity also leads to the formulation of a minimal normative criterion in hermeneutics: nonexclusion and the willingness to promote interaction. This criterion is critically related to the perpetual longing for differentiation in many genitive hermeneutics, a desire that leads people all too quickly to being closed and unwilling to interact—characteristics on which universalistic approaches are reproached. It is a normative criterion because it indicates that in which the quality of interpretation lies: in the search for continuing dialogue and the insights that correspond with it, i.e., the idea that understanding is always incomplete and vulnerable, the desire for inclusion, and the striving for consensus.

The most important observation resulting from the considerations discussed above is that if one investigates the much-cherished idea of "equality of interpretations," one comes to an unexpected result: taking this value seriously has the consequence that interpretations are *not* equal. Interpretations differ in the degree to which they are willing to learn from "strange" interpretations; the more they are willing to do so, the more valuable they are.

---

7. The norm for nonexclusion emerges from "the idea of 'human dignity' that is found on the abstract level of eccentricity where all people are equal in principle. It entails that people have the right to a minimum existence and to equal basic rights for their interactions. It also entails that, where power and making decisions are concerned, everyone can participate in principle. Exclusion from this on the basis of race, culture, gender, social position is not permitted." The second norm is willingness to promote interaction and is "linked to the actual differences between people on the empirical level and has, as a supplement to the former, a character related to content—promotion of interaction. It qualifies interhuman relationships, policy measures, social processes, cultural convictions on the basis of their positive or negative contribution to the interactive possibilities of groups and individuals" (Procee 1991).

Ethics and Interpretation: The Eschatological Dimension of Understanding

Our primary source regarding the ethical aspects of this final conclusion is Levinas. Wherever exclusion occurs, wherever interaction with the unfamiliar is not sought, the ethics of interpretation come into play. The insights of Levinas and others on the importance of that which is unfamiliar in interpretation processes are essential to the practice of encounter and interaction that we are committed to focus on. We will look further at these insights.

Levinas's work can be characterized as thinking in terms of lasting difference. Respect for what is unfamiliar is the foundation of this quality (Van Heijst 1995, 218; Cohn Eskenazi 2003, 145; Cohn Eskenazi, Phillips, and Jobling 2003). The unfamiliar, which manifests itself beyond my horizon, must be welcomed. Why? Because the unfamiliar—the other—is the only thing that can keep me from my perpetual longing for totality, for mastery. "It is not the insufficiency of the I that prevents totalization, but the Infinity of the Other," Levinas writes in his *Totality and Infinity* (1961, 8). Like his philosophy, Levinas's theory of interpretation is dominated entirely by ethics: first the ethics, then the interpretation. The orientation to the other has biblical roots. The eschatological orientation of the Tanakh becomes manifest at crucial points and is expressed in the orientation to "the other," to "elsewhere," and to "the otherwise." Already in Genesis 1, the relationship between infinity and fecundity is laid: "Be fertile and increase." In contrast to Odysseus, who returns home, Abraham is led elsewhere.[8] The whole of the Pentateuch is governed by eschatology.[9] Moses does not enter the promised land; others do. Thus, what Moses did, he did for others. The Tanakh ends midway through the sentence "and let him go up" (2 Chron. 36:23). The way the Hebrew Bible is conceived as open to the future, to what must still come, to beyond my time emphasizes the importance of infinity. It resists totality and shows the birth of a new possibility—an otherwise—and thus of the responsibility for it.

Orientation to the other in interpretation processes implies welcoming what every exegete in fact experiences—namely, that texts are polysemic, polyphonic, and diverse. Totality's opposition to infinity represents exclusion, or not welcoming the other.[10] The other is the enemy. Totality is not only destructive and leads to war—there are only enemies on the battlefield—but it is also untrue. Totality is not prepared to take texts' reserve of meaning into consideration; rather, it dehumanizes by erasing the particulars and reducing them to its own objective and ultimate meaning, regardless of the reality of the variety of possible meanings. The varied nature of the meaning of texts is continually sacrificed, always through an appeal to the supposed objective meaning.

---

8. Odysseus's return and homecoming represent the development of Western philosophy: "the identity, sameness, and egoism which is ultimately protected, not exiled, called outside, broken up."

9. See also the numerous articles by José Severino Croatto on the Pentateuch as a book of unfulfilled promises; see de Wit 1991; Severino Croatto 1982; 1991; 1994; 1997.

10. "Infinity" is the English translation of the original French *infini*, which has a meaning slightly different from the concept of infinity. *Infini* does not refer to a new system, now the opposite of totality, but means "open, unfinished"; there is still room for more and others.

In Levinas, infinity is not a vague concept, something without boundaries. On the contrary, it has to do primarily *with* boundaries and with going beyond them. Infinity is produced "by bound and bonded persons." "Infinity is produced in the relationship of the same with the other. It does not pre-exist" (Levinas 1961, 26). In other words, wealth and fertility in interpretation are not an *a priori* given but happen where one's own context-bound interpretation encounters the other's. When the self and the other offer to cross the boundary and interaction occurs, the striving for plenitude and transcendence and the diverse nature of the text cannot be reduced to being purely one's own. The other must be qualified, yet it is not so much the other in general; here, too, Levinas wants the Tanakh to have the deciding voice. The other is primarily the widow, the orphan, and the stranger.[11]

What does infinity imply for the attribution of meaning to texts?[12] Levinas argues that, in principle, there are at least as many readings as there are readers, for every reader brings his or her concerns, insights, perspectives, and experiences to the text and can read the text like a letter addressed to him or her. What a text can say depends on the multiplicity of readers and readings. If one wants to do justice to the striving for plenitude, if one wants to take seriously the eschatological— i.e., reading and interpretation "by the other," "elsewhere," and "otherwise"[13]—as a quality of the interpretation process, then each reader is irreplaceable. No reader can be missed. The truth of the text, the revelation of its mystery, lies therefore precisely in

> the contributions of a multiplicity of people: the uniqueness of
> each act of listening carries the secret of the text; the voice of
> Revelation, in precisely the inflection lent by each person's ear,
> is necessary for the truth of the Whole. . . . The multiplicity of
> people, each one of them indispensable, is necessary to produce
> all the dimensions of meaning; the multiplicity of meanings is
> due to the multiplicity of people.[14]

---

11. Van Heijst also argues in this vein: "In summary, I claim to have found two criteria for determining the value of the strange. The first criterion concerned breaking the monotone of culture, in which suppressed voices are coming to occupy positions for speaking. . . . The second criterion, tied to the first, was that the marginalized, who have no claims to power, have become authoritative. Levinas articulates this on the basis of his Jewish background by means of the biblical prototype of the other" (Van Heijst 1995, 233).

12. For the following see Cohen 2001, 249–50.

13. Levinas regauges the concept of eschatology—in his terms, metaphysics—in the biblical theological sense. Metaphysics, Levinas writes, "is that which is turned toward the 'elsewhere' and the 'otherwise' and the 'other'" (1961, 33). He thus lists three central concepts in the Hebrew Bible. "The 'elsewhere' can describe the Hebrew Bible's predominant shape as striving to reach elsewhere—the promised land, which is but a hope both at the end of the Torah and at the end of the entire Hebrew canon (see 2 Chr 36: 22–23); the 'otherwise' appears as the prophetic critique and its messianic aspirations; the 'other' leads to the otherness of God and fellow humans who must be encountered in the face-to-face meeting!"

14. Cohen 2001, 249, the quote is from E. Levinas, "Revelation in Jewish Tradition," in *The Levinas Reader* 1989, 159.

To reiterate, for Levinas, ethics is the concept that determines proper reading. This can be seen in the four standards that he employs for what he calls "ethical exegesis": (1) concrete and productive integration of spirit and letter; (2) pluralism of readers and readings; (3) virtue and existential self-transformative wisdom; and (4) sensitivity to authority in the sense that people when reading the Hebrew Bible understand that in doing so they are actualizing an *ethical*-religious tradition (Cohen 2001, 248ff.).

In the event of nonintegration of spirit and letter, reading can become such a game that it leads to "angelic dreaminess" and the complete neglect of historical situations of suffering and exclusion. The ethical has priority in the integration of letter and spirit. What traces of suffering and of human experience are seen in or behind the text? What traces are now visible in the light of the text?

Multiplicity is therefore not a defect, as suggested by those who claim to employ epistemological laws that actually only appear in mathematics. No, the diversity in readers and readings is a tribute to the continuing revelation and, hermeneutically stated, to the continual unfolding of the texts' potential for meaning.

The dialogical dimension of interpretation, of listening to others—to old and new readers—prevents the interpreter from standing on the sidelines unwilling to dirty his hands. The statement in the Talmud that using sacred texts makes clean hands dirty should also be understood in this sense. According to Levinas, proper reading produces transformation, engagement, and passion for the concern of the texts in the interpreter: "Exegesis lives," Levinas writes, "because it engages the lives of those who engage in it." Thus, for Levinas, exegesis is more than historically oriented critical reflection on what texts could have meant in their original settings. No, he is concerned with ethical exegesis and defines the work of exegetes in line with what South African and Latin American exegetes call "socially engaged biblical scholars."[15] "This exegesis," he writes, "makes the text speak, while critical philology speaks of the text. The one takes the text to be a source of teaching; the other treats it as a thing."

To read texts from the Hebrew Bible is to enter an old house, an old tradition. People connect themselves to a tradition "as old as the world," i.e., "as old as the humanity of the human" (Hand 1989, 255). However varied and diverse this tradition is, it is an ethical-religious tradition with a past that is oriented to the future and to peace. What is continually at stake in this tradition is the future of the earth and the humanity of being human. Reading these texts, in conjunction with old and new readers, also implies responsibility for making this ethical tradition current—for keeping alive this tradition that is realized in the discussion on law (in the form of the Torah), justice, and peace (Hand 1989, 196). The miracle of the Bible, and—as Cohen supplements Levinas—of all religious texts, does not lie in a common literary origin of the texts but in the fact that these texts

---

15. Gerald West defines socially engaged biblical scholars in terms of "the participation of the biblical scholar in forms of social transformation. The biblical scholar who is called to interpret the Bible with ordinary poor and marginalised communities is usually one who is already involved in forms of social struggle, reconstruction, and development, and who already has taken sides with the poor and marginalised in their struggles for survival, liberation and life" (West 1997: 99–100).

merge into the same fundamental content—namely, the ethical. How then, from a hermeneutical view, can one speak about peace in light of irreducible diversity and variety of the readers and the texts? Peace, Levinas would say, is not universal sameness but an ethical answer to alterity (otherness); justice consists in recognizing that the other is always other than what we see of him or her.

Organized Confrontation

We will now conclude our attempt to make use of Levinas for the topic that occupies us.[16] Procee, Levinas, and many others emphasize—each in his own distinct way—the fundamental importance of nonexclusion, respect for others, and interaction. The process of interpreting Bible texts becomes richer to the extent that its irreducible eschatological dimension is honored and that other readers who read in other places and in other ways are involved in the discussion of the ethical implications of these texts.

But are readers prepared to do so just like that? When we ask Western exegetes how orientation to the elsewhere, the other, and the otherwise is given shape in their exegesis, the answer is a meager one. Hardly anything has come of a systematic interaction with, for example, colleagues from Latin America or Africa, where the elsewhere and the otherwise are often a given (de Wit 2008; Huning 2005, 102–3).[17] The same is true, for that matter, of the mutual interaction between

---

16. We lack the space here to take up the question of how respect for the other, how radical alterity (otherness), is related to the possibility of encounter. It is a much discussed topic in Levinas's philosophy. Ricoeur is critical, precisely on that point: "Levinas is guilty of treating a non-relation as a relation." Levinas's views on otherness should be read as a hyperbole, a deliberate exaggeration, according to Ricoeur. Cohen points out that there can be a certain encounter between the self and the other in Levinas. Ricoeur does not look enough at what Levinas says about the familial aspect of the self as created, born within the "family of men." "The self is susceptible to radical otherness because it is a being that is born, born from and into a web of familial relations." In part 4 of *Totality and Infinity* there are fine examples given by Levinas of the self's "capacity of reception," according to Cohen. "There the separated self—the self susceptible to moral relations—is determined as capable of moral encounter precisely because of its created rather than its caused or posited being." Cf. Cohen 2001, 298ff. Following Ricoeur, Annelies van Heijst sees Levinas's holding to radical otherness as "wishful thinking": "I do not read Levinas' work as a realistic description of what actually happens in the ethical situation: it is 'wishful thinking' or a metaphorical description that invites one to look and act differently" (Van Heijst 1995, 218).

17. At the end of the 1980s E. S. Gerstenberger concluded that the differences between what was discussed in the *Zeitschrift für die Alttestamentliche Wissenschaft* between 1965 and 1984 and the topics that Latin American exegetes discussed in those years were gigantic. Whereas the Latin Americans were much occupied with topics such as oppression, poverty, exclusion, suffering, liberation, joy, and gratitude, *ZAW* paid scarcely any attention to such topics. On this and the question of relevance in exegetical research see my *Leerlingen van de Armen* (1991, 161 and elsewhere). If a similar investigation were conducted now, two decades later, the same conclusion would probably be reached. The well-known exegetical journal *Revista de Interpretación Bíblica Latinoamericana (RIBLA)* is a model for how a number of Latin American exegetes give shape to their engagement. A central theme—relevant for the Latin American situation—is continually discussed from different perspectives, using different Bible texts, and by different authors. Thus in the last ten years the following topics can be found: economy and the full life (*economía y vida plena*, 1998); the poor (1999); dignity (*dignidad*) (particularly of women), the year of jubilee and hope/utopia, rereading the prophets, asymmetry of power (*asimetría de poderes*), religion and erotica, utopia in everyday life, reading Luke from the perspective of the experience of the poor,

African and Latin American exegetes and so many other groups. It is difficult for exegetes to escape from dominant reading traditions and to be filled with an ongoing responsibility for reading "with" others. Nonetheless, interaction and confrontation are necessary for Bible reading to be transforming.

Here, we stumble on one of the challenges that the our research will take up. Cultural diversity will be introduced as a hermeneutical factor, and confrontation will be organized. In practice, this means that groups of Bible readers from radically different situations will be connected and brought into discussion on the meaning of the Bible text that they will read together. Here, intercultural stands for interaction. The concept *cultural* is used because of the fundamental meaning of culture in people's mental programming. This is therefore not interreligious hermeneutics but intercultural hermeneutics in a religious perspective, for it concerns Bible texts, i.e., texts that many people experience as fundamental for their existence and view of the world.

Further Empirical Research

Before we finally move on to the Andes or the rice paddies of Asia, we should return for a moment to the question of empirical research. We sketched above the contours of the code system for the first phase of the reading process, in which groups read in their own situation, without any encounter with others. In the second phase, groups are connected, and interaction—the intercultural discussion of the religious text—can occur. We consider this interaction to be fundamental, to be a quality that is a minimum normative criterion for proper reading. But how does the formulation of theory occur? Can it also be established empirically if this minimum normative criterion is not met? Our answer is affirmative. Just as in the first phase, a code system can be developed that is sensitive to this situation. In the existing code system, there are all kinds of theological-hermeneutical components; those familiar with the material will discover how much we have consulted cultural studies, sociology, anthropology, and empirical research into intercultural communication (de Wit 2004a, 395–436).

Central questions asked of the empirical material are: Has there been development and growth or stagnation and freezing? Also, the code system is very much directed at the analysis of the interaction with the partner group; how do the readers deal with the partner group as such? What is the effect of the interaction? The code system is divided here, again, into three main categories.

The First Main Category. In this category, supplementary information is collected about the two partnering groups. A varied composition can be established. Motivation, intercultural experience, and expectations are examined again. All of this information is constantly brought into relationship with the information about the partner group, which is now known and of which the givens also have

---

the psalms and the poor, Jesus the Healer; empire (imperio), healing of the body, the Bible movement in Latin America (50th issue (2005)), etc. For a discussion and evaluation of difference between Latin American and European/North American biblical studies see also, for example, my article "Lezen met Jael" (de Wit 2001).

been coded. There is a strong reliance here on the results and information from the first phase.

The Second Main Category. This is an extremely important category. Here, the partner groups' interaction with each other is mapped. Do people acquire any knowledge of the partner group's context? Do they address the partner group directly ("Dear Partner Group")? Or do people continue to objectify and to think in essentialisms? Is there a "culture/co-culture" (poor/rich) communication pattern as described and analyzed by Paulo Freire? What role do power and asymmetry play in the communication? Is there interest in the profile of the partner group? Are certain features of the partner group striking (vulnerability, experiences of suffering, ethnic background, openness)? What attitude do people themselves take—critical, "mindful," "nonjudgmental," open, vulnerable? Is there tolerance for ambiguity in the belief system of the partner group, or do people only want something from the partner group that they themselves cannot supply—namely, absolute coherence and logic? Do people want to convert the other reader(s) to their vision of the significance of the text?

At the same time, the hermeneutical-exegetical aspect of the interaction is coded: What differences or similarities does each group itself (and then also the researcher) discover with regard to method, focalization, identification patterns, appropriation, and the way the text is made relevant by the partner group and embedded in their own lives? How do people deal with these similarities and differences? Do the similarities and differences lead to an "ecumenical honeymoon"? Do people deal with differences in the way that anthropology calls "graceful fighting"?[18] Are differences "blunted" through, for example, an appeal to "religious universals"—we are, after all, brothers and sisters, and there is one God—or do they lead to a break and rejection?

The Third Main Category. In this category, the code system is directed toward analyzing and establishing the effect of the groups' interaction. We will explore which factors are influential in the freezing and thawing of faith insights. In the code system, "freezing" is also called, to use a term employed by Droogers and others, a "return to one's own repertoire"; "thawing" is also called "growth."

The codes that are valid here are, for example, the following: Does a process occur that Bar-Tal has called the transition from cognitive discrepancy to cognitive consensus? If so, which of the four factors cited by Bar-Tal play or do not play a role in this process: Recognition of Relativism; Satisfaction of Needs; Salient and Significant Information; Third Party Intervention (Bar-Tal 1990)? What has then happened to a person's own view of the text? Is there growth? If so, why and on the basis on which factors? Is there rejection of the reading of the partner group? If so, why and on the basis of which factors? Is there an increase in intercultural competence (insight into the cultural determination of a group's own values and those of the partner group), a relativization of one's own insights, or a

---

18. Graceful fighting is a certain way of handling differences and is nourished by the conviction that "if we can live together in community, then someday we shall be able to resolve our conflicts." The view here is that conflict belongs to community. That is in line with Martin Buber, who does not see community as a group in complete harmony but "community is a group that can handle conflict."

development of a so-called "third-culture perspective"? Or is there "culture shock" and a return to one's own repertoire?

Because our research is concerned with intercultural communication in religious perspective, in the analysis we will pay attention primarily to what the communication between groups does to the beliefs of those involved. Here we will look not only at how the relationship between gospel and culture develops in this process[19] but also at growth and stagnation in faith insights. The terms used here are derived largely from manuals and studies on intercultural communication. In our research, we will use religious variants of the terms, and we will attempt to make visible the special role of faith in processes of intercultural communication.

Here is an example. Where cultural studies speak of a third-culture perspective, we will use this term in a hermeneutical-religious sense and then analyze whether the learning process has enriched the group or broadened its horizon. Has the faith of the group members become deeper? Are people freer with respect to their own faith tradition? Is there a richer, more creative, liberated way of reading and reflecting on one's own faith? Has a new perspective developed, nourished by the interaction with the partner group and the longing for a new "third" look at the text and the praxes manifested in the text?

When sociologists speak about a third-culture perspective, they do so in optimistic terms, and the contours of the new person become visible. The third-culture man/woman is

- "open-minded toward new ideas and experiences,"
- feels "empathy toward people from other cultures,"
- has "a more accurate perception of differences and similarities between the host culture and his/her own,"
- is sooner able "to describe behavior he/she doesn't understand than to evaluate unfamiliar behavior as bad, nonsensical, or meaningless,"
- is better able "to detect role behaviors,"
- is better equipped "to establish meaningful relationships with people from the other cultures,"
- is "less ethnocentric" (Gudykunst and Kim 2003).

Here we encounter the new, mature world citizen. He or she is able to deal with cultural differences and is not ethnocentric. The special content of our analysis—key values of the Christian tradition such as compassion, solidarity, forgiveness, acceptance of the other—is delineated in contrast with the more general skills that anthropology, sociology, and culture studies emphasize. If central texts of the Christian tradition are involved in intercultural discussion in a religious perspective, concepts other than autonomy, cultural sensitivity, and independent and critical thinking also appear to play a fundamental role. The Third Perspective immediately becomes ethically charged; it becomes a Third Faith Perspective nourished by the longing for the kingdom of God. It is a perspective that is also

---

19. Are, for example, culturally operative values overruled by faith insights that are introduced by partner groups? One could think here of Geert Hofstede's depth dimensions of culture clustered in: dealing with power, with tradition, with that which threatens and is new, with the perception of male/female roles, with collectivism/individualism, etc.

eschatologically loaded and within which power differential (asymmetry, inequality), premature death, and oppression are determinative. Concepts such as justice, guilt, love, liberation, one's neighbor, and redemption carry the discussion on the differences.

A profile can be constructed from the reading reports and displayed on a graph. I will give a few examples.

The following illustration shows the coding process. The researcher looks at the material from different perspectives; a text segment (quotation) can be assigned different codes because it contains several components.

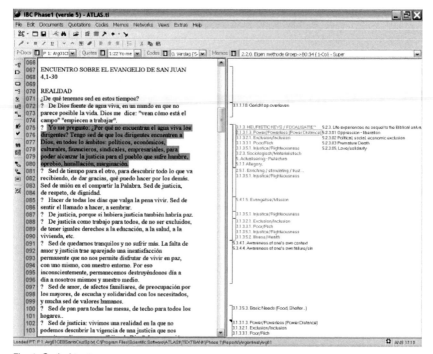

Fig. 1. Coded text.

The profile of one group can be determined on the basis of specific aspects of the interpretation process and compared with that of another group. The explanation strategies of the text are coded for both groups below. How have the groups dealt with the explanation of the text, with its historical background, the original language, the literary and theological aspects of the text, the narrative and rhetorical structure of the text, the further literary context, etc.? The illustrations below show the profile of two partner groups, a Dutch ecumenical group and a Nicaraguan Pentecostal group. The scores diverge greatly. The Dutch group is very occupied with exegesis and scores much higher on this part than its partner group. Both reports can be compared, for they are about the same size and have a similar number of coded quotations. A so-called network view shows the differences immediately. Figures 2 and 3 indicate how much the Dutch group is

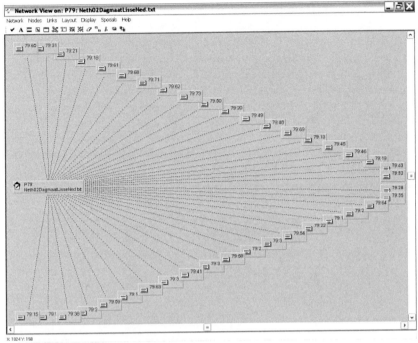

Fig. 2. Network view of Dutch reading report.

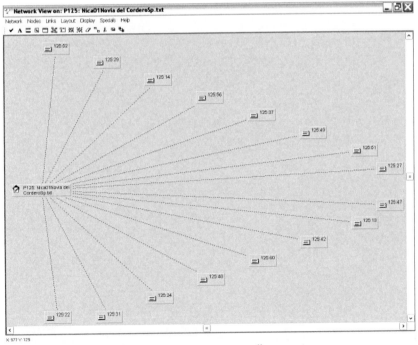

Fig. 3. Network view of Nicaraguan partner group reading report.

occupied with understanding the text and how much less that is the case with the Nicaraguan partner group.

If we look at how the groups make the text relevant to the present time, the situation is precisely the opposite. It is now the Nicaraguan group whose scores are high. It is then interesting and impressive to see how the groups approach and show great appreciation for each other in the interaction phase. Looking through the eyes of the other, the groups become aware of their own way of reading and discover that the method and interpretation of the partner group complement their own.

We will leave our short description of the analysis of the empirical material at that. It constitutes part of our attempt to contribute to theory formation and the development of a new method of reading the Bible.

3

Ordinary Readers

We must now make the trips we promised we would. All the foregoing remarks on the effect of texts on the actions of human beings, on interaction as a quality of interpretation, on empirical research, and on the ethical dimension of understanding lead us to an area that is essential for our study: the world of the ordinary reader of Bible stories.

That is the space in which the connections among culture, context, tradition, and reading become visible—more so than they do in the world of the professional reader. Here we encounter a concept—referred to in Spanish as *lectores comunes*—that is used a great deal but is not easy to define. I will return to that shortly. Let us first look at who populates the space in which we are so interested. I will provide a few portraits.

This is Maruge from Kenya, perhaps the oldest pupil in the world, in his school uniform, with shorts on.

Maruge from Kenya

The caption of the newspaper article reads, "When President Kibaki introduced free primary education in 2003, the illiterate great-grandfather Maruge seized his chance. His reason for

A group from the Netherlands

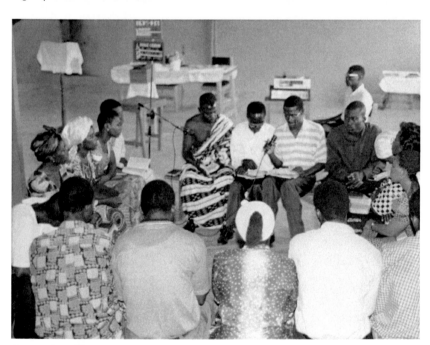

A group from Ghana

A group from Bolivia, with gifts from the Dutch partner group (note the yellow bag "Blijvend Scherpe Prijzen" ("Permanent Low Prices") [Photo: Victor Huacani]

A group of Aymara women from Bolivia [Photo: Photo caroline]

A group of Korean students

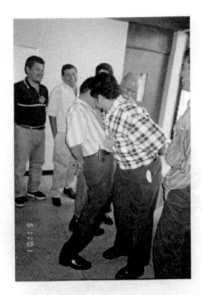

CARLOS (SAMARITANA) ES TOCADO POR
FRANCISCO (JESÚS), LOS OTROS
SE RÍEN Y SE BURLAN

A group from El Salvador: Carlos (the Samaritan woman) is touched by Francisco (Jesus). The others laugh and make jokes.

starting school at this age was, 'I suspected that a preacher did not understand the Bible very well. Therefore, I wanted to learn to read myself.'"[1]

There they are: the ordinary readers who populate our area of research. Most of the photos come from a major project, Through the Eyes of Another: Intercultural Reading of the Bible (2001–2004), that is now being continued through the Dom Hélder Câmara Chair. Small groups of Bible readers read a Bible story together, first in their own situation and then communally, as a small group. Finally, they are brought into contact with a partner group (far away or close by) and begin discussing the meaning of the text with that group.[2] They attempt to look at the text again through the eyes of another.

---

1. Photo ANP, in the daily *Trouw.*
2   We had long discussions about how to link the groups. Finally we decided to use only three criteria for selection, from what had become a long list: not the same country, not the same church, not the same social status.

4

The Reserve of Meaning

Knowing about the hermeneutical diversity of Christianity on a theoretical level is one thing; seeing how it works in practice is another. If one wants to see Levinas's concept of infinity at work, to understand the postmodern emphasis on fluidity and the reserve of meaning in texts, to be aware of the ethical implications of interpretation, and to discover how the Holy Scripture can function, then one must set up a project like this one. Why are we so delighted? Because we have seldom enjoyed our discipline as much as we did when the first reading reports arrived and we discovered that each one brought new insights and questions, and a different way of looking at the text. While concerns about the challenges of asymmetry, inequality, premature death, and poverty press upon one so much in the practice of intercultural reading, the possibilities that the Holy Scripture offers for discussions on peace and justice encourage us and give us hope. Entering this space is like entering holy ground. Latin American and African biblical theologians are right when they speak of a certain mysticism in such forms of communal Bible reading. It is, in a word, fantastic!

I must share some examples. I will organize the empirical material—the 3,000 pages of "peoples' commentary"—around a few key concepts that we have just looked at and show how they work in practice. In the end, I will come back to who and what ordinary readers are.

Alterity (Otherness) and Infinity in Hermeneutical Perspective

We will turn to the story that was read by all participants, the story in John 4 of the meeting between Jesus and the Samaritan woman at Jacob's well. We will look at what readers from radically different contexts do with this story.

But first the story. A tired man sits alone next to a well in the foothills. It is hot, and he is thirsty; he needs help. There is water available—he is sitting next to a well—but he has no jar, and the well is deep. A woman from the village comes, alone, to draw water; we never learn her name. She is thirsty as well. The man and the woman have never seen each other before. What they share is their thirst and a common past. There are great differences between them: he is a man and she is a woman; they come from different peoples. The man has crossed the border to get to the well; his people do not usually come to where he is now sitting. His people despise her people. The man speaks to her and asks for water. She can help quench his thirst because she has a jar with her. But she does not. Instead, she asks him, "Why are you speaking to me? Your people do not speak to us!" That changes everything. A conversation ensues about thirst and water, about who they actually are and the tradition from which they come, about wholeness and healing. Something fundamental happens to both. He interrupts his journey and goes to her home and her people. She changes her life; she does not have to flee from her past. She begins to testify. They will never forget each other.

5

How Differences Arise: Domains of Reference

Roland Barthes once wrote that the stories of the world are innumerable. How people arrange and apply narrative patterns in stories also seems to be infinite, because the number of factors that mediate in the process of attributing meaning is so large. Infinity is not only a philosophical concept that evokes what Levinas calls ethical exegesis; it also is a technical concept. Between the hard grammatical details of the ancient text and the contemporary understanding of it is a ceaseless process that generates differences. Such differences arise because of new exegetical insights and methods but have to do primarily with the texts' capacity to illuminate situations not seen by the author, which are then projected back onto the text and result in a new understanding of its meaning. The greatest differences—"otherness" in its most radical form—are manifested in efforts to understand the references of old made by the text and in efforts to make them relevant for the current historical moment. Viewed from the perspective of the contemporary reader, references made by Bible texts are often vague, incomplete, and fragmentary. Every text has its narrative gaps, simply because not everything can be said. Variation thus appears primarily in what is not said by the text. In that sense, one might say that the texts do nothing but ask for completion by the reader's imagination. That completion is always an adventure: the ancient texts never say whether completion is allowed. This completion process is also making the text relevant for the present.

But when a text is made relevant to today's world, its original reference to its own sociohistorical reality is replaced by a new one—ours. It is primarily the fact that the processes of making the text relevant to today are context bound that generates radical otherness. Appealing to cognitive psychology, which studies the comprehension of texts, Bruce Malina referred to the importance of the so-called "scenario model for hermeneutics" (Sanford and Garrod 1981). The reader's understanding of a text develops primarily through searching for recognizable domains of reference—scenarios—in which the text wants to place the reader and itself assumes a position. "This domain of reference will be rooted in some model of society and of social interaction," Malina writes. Thus the domain of reference is always social and historical and invites the reader to recognize and construct an analogy.[1] The point here is that the interpreter's set of domains of reference is limited and is also always strongly influenced by his or her own context.[2] In other words, the analogy that the contemporary interpreter is able to construct between contemporary domains of reference and those of the text depends very much on his or her situation. And the combination of the narrative gaps and the contextually determined handling of a text's reference is a primary source of differences.

Alterity

We will look at different domains of reference that readers of Bible stories have and at the traces these leave in the empirical material. We will examine otherness and its hermeneutical effect—infinity.

Differences are manifested on all levels and in all phases of the interpretation process. In our research, some groups have been very sober with respect to the liturgical setting, while others have used all kinds of symbolic objects and composed their own songs. We read in a report from Nigeria:

> The group members bring along with them such symbolic
> objects as bottled water, a cross, a candle, and pieces of white
> cloth. The group considers these objects symbolic of life, pu-

---

1. See Bruce Malina 1983, 11–25. The scenario model considers the text to be a sequence of explicit and implicit scenes or schemas "in which the mental representation evoked in the mind of the reader consists of a series of settings, episodes, or models deriving directly from the mind of the reader, coupled with appropriate alterations to these settings, episodes, or models as directed by the text." The reader must carry out two tasks: identify via the text the appropriated reference domain (look at the appropriated scene, the scheme or model that is suggested by the text) and then, as far as possible, within this "domain of reference," determine the position that the text wants to occupy in it; see Malina 1983, 13–14, with an appeal to Sanford and Garrot 1981). "The point to be underscored is that if interpretation of a written language of any sort takes place a domain of reference will be used by the reader. This domain of reference will be rooted in some model of society and of social interaction" (Malina 1983: 16).
2. In *Her Master's Tools*, Caroline Vander Stichele points to the problems of analogy, as formulated and used by Ernst Troeltsch, Adolf von Harnack, and many other historical-critical biblical scholars, as an epistemological principle of history. History was to be known via analogy, but the analogy, as epistemological principle, was nourished by post-Enlightenment Germany and analogy can only be construed where in this context analogous experience with, for example, the biblical domains of reference is available. The number of scenarios that are available is limited and works as a filter, always leveling history out and adapting it to the present. See Vander Stichele 2005, 10ff. In *The Reality of the Historical Past*, Paul Ricoeur points emphatically to the fact that remembering always has the form of analogy and is thus never a copy of what it remembers but is always a reenactment of it. "Summing up the whole itinerary of the present study, I would say that the recourse to analogy acquires its full sense only against the backdrop of the dialectic of Same and Other: the past is re-enacted in the mode of the identical. But it is so only to the extent that it is also what is absent from all of our constructions. The analogue, precisely, holds within it the force of re-enactment and of distancing, to the extent that being as is both being and not being" (Ricoeur 1985, 35–36).

rity, and light, which Christ radiates in the lives of Christians, etc. In addition, symbolic objects such as the "Ikenga" or "Ofo," cowries, clay pots, fowl feathers, and other objects of worship believed to be accepted by the ancestors in the African cultural setting are brought by members of the group.

A Dutch group brought "a lump of clay, a wedding ring and marriage certificate, a statue of two women, a wine glass, a weighing scale, binoculars, a swan, a pocket calendar, and a nameplate."

The composition of the groups; the origin, social status, and church background of the participants; the places where they meet—all of these differ radically. The groups have come from more than a hundred different denominations and more than twenty-five countries. So many different occupations have been represented that we could have built a whole new society. Shoemakers and masons have taken part, as have truck drivers and concrete workers, teachers of theology, ministers and priests, managers and cleaners, secretaries and artists, nurses and musicians, and unemployed and retired people. One of the Cuban groups reported the participation of a number of deaf-mute individuals. The places where people have met are diverse—in large historical churches, in the open air under palm trees, in slums, and on university campuses, for example.

Both the group dynamic and the method used in reading are culture specific. "Meetings always begin with a hymn, after members have had the opportunity to greet and inform about their health. One of the members leads in prayer and asks the blessing of the Lord on the procedures," wrote the reporter for the women's group in Kwazulu Natal, South Africa. The Cuban group wrote: "All meetings start with a liturgical time: chants, hymns, group exercises, prayers." A Dutch group reported:

> The chairwoman begins by reading a poem by African women.
> She then explains the intention of the meeting once again.
> Then the participants, who do not all know one another,
> introduce themselves.

There was a remarkable difference between groups in the Northern Hemisphere and those in the Southern Hemisphere with regard to their willingness to go on the adventure of making a text relevant to the present time. Northern groups hesitated, wrestled, and were restrained and aloof; southern groups jumped at the story and often identified immediately with a character in it. We saw an example of this difference in the paragraphs above. Hans Snoek has explored this difference in the degree of appropriating the text and also has shown that there are significant differences in focalization. "Whereas the 'Third World' groups paid relatively much attention to John 4:7–15, in the Netherlands only two groups looked extensively at the metaphor [of living water]" (Snoek 2004, 189ff.). A good example of the relationship between context and focalization can be found in the report of a Nigerian group:

> The reading of the text (John 4) evoked interesting thoughts, memories, and experiences from the individual lives of the members of this group. The verses reminded the members of diverse aspects of African cultural values and practices—namely, ancestorhood, the problem of the "Osu" system in Igboland, polygamy, hospitality, and womanhood/motherhood. Though the group read all the verses of the chapter, it however carefully studied the verses that related to each of the above African values and practices.

The status of the text varies a great deal in each group. While some groups approach the text with suspicion and critical questions and begin to deconstruct it immediately, other groups approach it with trust and respect.

The life stories of the participants display profound differences: "I am 38 years old," a participant from Ghana wrote. "I have eight children, and my husband divorced me away." The Indian group wrote, "All the members of the group are Dalits, the socially depressed classes of India. They have been deprived of dignity for thousands of years." A group of transsexuals in India also took part:

> This group of transsexuals is not Christian. Bible studies, prayers, retreats, etc., are conducted for them by a Christian priest. . . . They are not allowed entry into schools and colleges, which is also one of the important reasons why eighty percent of transsexuals in India are engaged in the flesh trade.

The South African Group made the following portrait of their group: "The average age of the group is sixty plus. Most of the members are married and have children who are independent grown-ups already. All members of the group, except J., who lives on a wine farm, live in upper-middle-class residential areas in S."

Infinity

Where does otherness lead if people read the same Bible story? The empirical material shows how infinity is given form. The narrative and rhetorical structure of the story elicits an unlimited number of answers. While some groups discover syntactic and literary connections, other groups do not notice them. The answers to the internal reading dynamic of the text are extremely varied. However much semioticians like Umberto Eco emphasize that texts have an internal dynamic and a primary meaning, their ability to lead readers along a defined, fixed path appears to be limited. Readers do not always read the whole text. What people find striking in the text varies by group.

The encounter with infinity is overwhelming. Almost every reading report shows how aspects of the text are illuminated, matters are discussed, and connections are seen in ways that are unique to that group. The different groups not only reflect on entirely different sections of the text than other groups, they also differ fundamentally with regard to what is in the text: the morality of the Samaritan woman (whore, sinner, victim); Jesus' attitude (paternalistic, loving, strict); the function of the well (meeting place, place where prostitutes can legally have sex with their clients, sacred ground); and the time of the meeting (is the woman looking for an affair, and is Jesus also looking for an affair)? Does she want to avoid other people? The groups' perspectives differ on everything.

Janet Dyk investigated reading reports from sixteen countries and fifty-seven groups and raised the question of what meaning the groups gave to "living water." She found no fewer than fifty different meanings (Dyk 2004b, 377–94; 2004a, 218–42). Living water as message, as gospel, as Word of God, as the Holy Spirit, as an image of personal faith, as redemption, as Jesus himself, as the kingdom. But the literal, physical meaning also appeared: water moving and flowing.[3]

Aukje Hoekema analyzed the meaning the groups gave to John 4:22 ("for salvation is from the Jews"). Here as well, fundamental differences appeared. For some, salvation represented rescue from sins; for others, rescue from a dire situation; and yet for others, Jesus himself was salvation. Were these differences regionally determined? No, the researcher concluded: the greatest differences were determined by the readers' varying theological and church backgrounds (Hoekema 2004, 171–88).

The agent, the Samaritan woman, was characterized in more than twenty different ways: as whore, victim, feminist, evangelist, sinner, ostracized/outcast, widow, seductress, etc.

Culture is an important factor in interpretation. Whether the text is successful in leading the reader to an analogous sociocultural domain depends very much on the reader's context. The Nigerian group reflected on the figure of Jacob and saw an ancestor, a discovery hardly shared by Western groups. Not all groups noted that the sixth hour—the hottest part of the day—plays an important role in the story. What is the meaning of the question, "Will you give me a drink?" In Brazil, the response was, "You cannot refuse anyone water," but in the Netherlands, it was, "Jesus does not have any right to ask her this." Does Jesus' brusque command, "Go, call your husband" mean that the woman "must first tell the truth—only then would she be free," as the group of Filipino ex-prostitutes read the story? Or is the Ghanaian reading correct, i.e., that Jesus wanted to say to her, "The one you are married to has not performed the marriage rites"?

Like a number of other groups, an Indian group felt that the fact that Jesus and the Samaritan woman were alone at the well was special. What made it extra special, according to this group, was that the meeting concerned someone from a high caste and a woman from a low caste, or perhaps a casteless person. In India, it is completely unusual for two people from different groups to speak privately with each other without shouting or giving orders.

For some groups, Jesus was primarily the Son of God, whereas for other groups he was primarily a thirsty, helpless man. Some groups saw problems that could not be solved—words, concepts, and narrative sequences that did not fit

---

3. A Salvadoran group reads the story entirely in the erotic key and gives the "living water" that Jesus offers an erotic meaning as well. "Yo no soy de aquí, si usted quiere (en tono de confidencia, se acerca) le doy de un agüita que yo tengo. Después de que la pruebe, ya no va querer tomar de otra." See also Dyk's remarks on the erotic meaning of "living water" in Song of Songs 4:15 (Dyk 2004, 228).

with their own logic: What does it say in the original? Other groups solved all problems by means of pregiven, Christian—for example, christological—schemas: all mysteries of the texts are unveiled through one basic concept, such as predestination, or God's omnipotence or omniscience.

Whereas many groups spent a great deal of time on the question of why Jesus had to go to Samaria ("Wasn't that actually cowardly?" a reading group participant remarked), the answer was immediately divine providence: "He had (God arranged it) to go to Samaria; that was predestined because there was a people thirsting for God . . . " The text is flattened into the echo of one's own dogmatic understanding. The story becomes one-dimensional.

One can easily become lost in the examples and in a microscopic analysis of factors that determine differences. That is a useful exercise: it is possible to map a number of central factors such as culture, church affiliation, faith tradition, and biography. However, because the combination of mediating factors is complex and in almost every case unique, one can ask about the extent to which one can and wishes to go with the empirical research. The task of intercultural hermeneutics is primarily to offer insight into the degree to which people are prisoners of dominant reading traditions. It offers them the possibility of objectifying those traditions and becoming capable of offering a salutary answer to the differences. It is important that the differences not be reduced to factors that are responsible for them but that they be seen in their hermeneutical significance—namely, as a long series of reading possibilities of one and the same text and as contributions to its meaning—as a tribute by readers to the text.

6

The Ethical Dimension of Intercultural Hermeneutics: Asymmetry

The Eschatological Caveat. The encounter with infinity leads to the above-mentioned insight that texts are inexhaustible. Even if repetitions can be seen throughout the centuries in dealing with narrative patterns, with the central message(s) of the text, each process of attributing meaning receives its own unique form via the particularity of the individual life of the reader who wants to appropriate the text. We have called this the eschatological dimension of the process of understanding. On the one hand, each reader appropriates the text in his or her own unique way; that is the gift of the text to the reader. On the other hand, all kinds of elements in the textuality of the text escape closure; they simply cannot be arranged in a scheme or resolved through historical or literary research.

In that sense one can agree with Derrida that each reader builds up a debt with regard to the text and with Levinas that the text is truly the Other. The text is always more than the reader. The particular, concrete text always contains a surprise for the reader. Every time that readers "log on" to the text, they confirm their dependence on it and debt to it (Phillips 1994, 283–325). It is also for this reason that philosophers like Gadamer emphasize so much the character of interpretation as play. Play is opposed here to seizures of power and to the utilitarian use of texts: the proper meaning is the one that serves. Texts are never the property of one reader. Interpretation is not the interrogation of a prisoner but the play of the "double gift"—what we earlier called "double transformation": something happens to the text and to the reader. The text gives the reader a unique gift—a new moment of self-understanding. In turn, the reader's gift to the text is the recognition of its vitality and infinity, and the fact that it is experienced as fundamental for one's own existence.

For readers who want to be responsible for the text, the eschatological dimension of understanding also has a deep ethical meaning. If it is clear that the ultimate meaning of the text will be revealed only at the end, when all readers have spoken and no one has been excluded, then this means that every process of closure—every reading of the text that claims to be the only legitimate one and to have exhausted the text—is premature. Whenever a praxis is based on such a premature fixing of the meaning of a text and leads to terror, destruction, colonization, and exclusion, the ethical dimension of each process of understanding it emerges in a dramatic way.

Asymmetry. Intercultural hermeneutics emphasizes the ethical dimension of reading in yet another way. A minimum normative criterion for good reading is the willingness to interact—the encounter with the other—as we saw earlier. Because the discussions concern Bible texts, dimensions of depth emerge in these interactions. Readers experience these texts as fundamental for their own lives, and their lives meet on a level of depth in the light of the text. But it is precisely in that encounter that the most dramatic differences are manifested between rich and poor, long life and premature death, a respected existence and exclusion, and relative rest and persecution. Intercultural Bible reading functions as a mirror of tremendous asymmetry and inequality in the world. A few examples will clarify what I mean.

One of the Bolivian groups reported, "All participants come from the slums of El Alto and La Paz. They are poor and belong to Indian groups. These districts lack the fundamental conditions for a normal life." One Brazilian group said about its members, "With one exception, all participants have only an elementary school education."

In Colombia, a group reported that most of its participants had only sporadic opportunities to work: "No one has a steady job. Most work as salespeople in small neighborhood stores, others babysit their neighbors' children, still others are housewives and depend on the support of their children."

A Dutch group wrote:

> We live in a free country where freedom of speech is very
> important. Privacy is highly esteemed. We are rich; we can go
> on vacation often and also have the time for that. We have very
> good social services: if you are sick, lose your job or are too old
> to work, there is always an allowance through which you can
> make ends meet. It is also not necessary for parents to live with
> their children when they get old. They now have the financial
> means themselves to live independently or in homes. People are
> continually growing older: for them to reach the age of eighty-
> five or ninety is no longer exceptional. The development level is
> quite high, and everyone can receive a grant to study.

A Nigerian group formulated the relationship between its own social position and political power as follows: "As most of the members are either church leaders, military chaplains, teachers, or businessmen, or are in civil job positions, they consider themselves more as people in power with indirect political say in the society."

Another Dutch group wrote, "In the social and political area, there are hardly any tensions in our immediate environment. We live in a peaceful village."

Finally, a Ghanaian group reported, "The average income of the people forming the Bible study groups is around thirty-two US dollars a month, which is not enough to buy food for a family, let alone pay school fees or buy new clothes."

These examples make clear what I mean. Where otherness—now in the socioeconomic sense—becomes manifest as asymmetry, the ethical dimension of reading religious texts in intercultural perspective is dramatically underscored.

The Face of the Other. The intercultural discussion on Bible texts leads to dialogue on the in-depth dimensions of existence. In making this religious-ethical tradition relevant to the present day, it is inevitable that asymmetry and its ethical implications will come up. But there is still an element that reinforces the call to responsibility in this form of reading religious texts; in intercultural Bible reading, the other does not remain a vague, objectifiable category. No, the asymmetry is perceptible and tangible. People meet one another—literally as well—they hear each other's life stories and begin to say each other's names: "We are curious," a group from El Salvador wrote to its Dutch partner group, "about how you pronounce our Spanish names. We pronounce your names precisely as they are written."

Hidden Transcript, Social Memory, and Trauma Processing

A group of South African women wrote about their experience with intercultural Bible reading:

> We come to the Bible study to gain more knowledge of the Bible and God's purpose for our lives, to share our ideas, and to understand that people have different points of view, but most of all we share a lot of that what is good and honest within us. . . . This is not only a learning process, but also a healing process—spiritually and physically. (my italics)

Experiences of suffering are shared, people learn from one another, and there is a reference to healing. In this quotation perhaps lies one of the most important values of communal Bible reading in small groups. I am referring here to what follows below.

The Space of the Hidden Transcript. In the empirical material, a significant correlation can be found between "small group/intimacy," "trust," and healing. "We thus began a process of intercultural Bible reading. Carefully and enthusiastically. In search of trust and intimacy," Marianne Paas wrote (2004, 89). Another Dutch group wrote, "The discussion was sometimes very personal, and that was possible because we felt very *safe*." "All of the members spontaneously participated in the discussion *freely*," a group from Chennai (India) said. A group from Ghana remarked, "In sum, the group had an interesting time during the number of times we met. At every session, members *freely* expressed their opinions." A group from Cuba stated, "They also felt comfortable with this method because it gave them the opportunity of expressing themselves in *confidence and brotherhood,* in their humble or cultured way of saying things, without false theories . . ." "The cohesion in the group created a reading environment where everybody felt *free* to participate," reported a group from Stellenbosch, South Africa (my italics).

Latin American liberation theology and other theologies always emphasize the importance of the small group. Hélder Câmara once wrote about this as follows:

> A particularly effective way of helping the poor
> To right the situation
> Is to encourage them to set up grass-roots communities.
> For in these we find a community spirit
> That lives on the gospel and draws its strength from Christ.
> It is important that these communities should spring up
> And get together in unity,
> Not in order to trample on the rights of others,
> But to prevent others from trampling on their rights.
> Experience shows that it is easy for the powerful
> To crush, one, five, or even ten people.
> But no human force can crush a coherent community,
> For it is a living God who dwells there
> And listens to the outcry of his people.[1]

Much has been written about these small communities—in Latin America the so-called base Christian communities or *comunidades eclesiales de base* (CEBs)—as places where resistance to church hierarchy occurs and alternative faith communities arise. Much less has been written about the fact that they also are primarily places of healing.

In these small communities, the hidden transcript is given shape. This concept, derived from the sociologist Scott, has been made fruitful for biblical hermeneutics by the South African biblical theologian Gerald West (Scott 1990; West 1996, 34ff.). In addition to or over against what can be said officially and obtained as true officially (public transcript), the hidden transcript can be articulated in the small group. Ordinary readers can say to one another what they themselves hear in the biblical story. Sometimes a true counterculture arises. This process is delicate and fragile, and people come to know one another differently. A new strategy of encounter and reading comes into being; it is related critically to and complements not only the academic reading but also the petrified, faded readings of church tradition. What cannot be said emerges, what cannot be thought or felt is expressed, and people can doubt where doubt is not permitted. In the safe space

---

1. Dom Hélder Câmara, *Charismatic Renewal and Social Action: A Dialogue,* cited in Schipani and Wessels 2002:, 88.

of the small group, the longing for liberation, healing, redemption, and radical change appear to be stronger than all pregiven "Christian" schemas.[2]

Social Memory, Visceral Memories. Stories, often horrifying, staggering, and full of "memory," emerge in the intimacy of the small group. These stories and their interpretations by readers, primarily those who live on the periphery, can be understood sociologically and labeled by Halbwachs' concept of social memory. Social memory theory can be considered a branch of the sociology of knowledge that arises in situations in which shared orientations, norms, and worldviews break down and collapse because of deep differences. Social memory theory is nourished by situations where truth claims are viewed with suspicion and investigated with respect to the interests of those who advance them. It arises within a culture of suspicion, ideological critique, and the breakthrough of the understanding that interpretation—also of the past—and power are closely connected. Social memory theory focuses primarily on the question of the way memories of earlier communities are constitutive for current communities. The sociologist Maurice Halbwachs (1877–Buchenwald 1945) is considered to be the father of social memory theory; his book *La Mémoire Collective* (published posthumously) was a pioneering study (Halbwachs 1950).

The starting point of social memory theory is that memory is a social phenomenon and constitutive for a community (Kirk 2005, 2; Keightley 2005, 133). Halbwachs was interested in the social aspects of memory. He argued that memory is not, as is often thought, the most individual possession of a person; rather, memory cannot be separated from the social world in which it is given shape. Memory is always formed within a certain social environment. Halbwachs analyzed how the structure and internal dynamic of a group influence the memory of people who belong to the group. The social environment is indispensable for the possibility of remembering itself, for it always gives coherence to the memories. Memory and remembering are always embedded in a contemporary moment and thus transcend the individual experience. The group to which people belong is determinative for the memory that they wish to cherish.

> Memory is a source of group identity, and in the constant retelling and celebration of its past, memory serves the community's cohesion by strengthening the bonds between its members. (Kirk 2005, 20–21)

Remembering is nourished and kept alive by the group to which one belongs. If this group is abandoned, a process of "forgetting" is often set in motion.

---

2. "While the first response in many Bible study groups is often the 'missionary response' or the dogmatically 'correct' response—the public transcript—critical modes of reading enable ordinary people from poor and marginalized communities to begin to articulate their 'working' readings and theologies, what is incipient and usually deliberately hidden from public view. The latter is clearly dangerous; what is hidden from the dominant is hidden for good reason, and can and should only be openly owned in a context of trust and accountability. But within such a context, the intersection of community and critical resources enables the recognizing, recovering, and arousing of dangerous memories (Metz), subjugated knowledges (Foucault), and hidden transcripts" (West 1993).

"Forgetting" is thus not only a mental, individual question but the result of a change in social place.

Community and memory are mutually determinative. Living communities are communities of memory. Whenever an individual enters a community, he or she shares the memories of the community. Certain experiences from the past are considered by the community to be fundamental. They become a master narrative, a master memory. The relation between these master memories and the community that cherishes them is dynamic.

Social memory has both formative and normative aspects. It is formative in the way it invites people to praxis, incorporates and instructs new members, and keeps the community together. It is normative because the memory is exemplary for the group that remembers the past in this way. Memory is thus the basis for a unique whole of meanings and values. In the stories about a community's beginning, about the deeds of its heroes and the original experiences of its ancestors, one can find what defines the community and what the community will be. "In truth, memory's framework provides the community's overarching view of reality; it sets forth reality's fundamental order, character, and significance" (Keightley 2005, 133). Memories are always ethically laden. An important aspect of the effect of memories on the present is therefore their ability to mobilize communities. Particularly in situations of oppression, the memory of liberation is not only cherished by oppressed communities but also can lead to resistance by these communities.

This is not the place to reflect further on social memory theory and its significance for biblical studies (de Wit 2006, 283–314).[3] What concerns us now is that part of our empirical material mirrors a process that has begun in recent years in Latin America and elsewhere and that can be compared to one experienced by concentration camp survivors. Gérard Namer describes how survivors of the camps were able to construct a coherent whole of memories only after groups of survivors were formed. Through these groups, the fragmented, inexpressible, and traumatic experiences of the camps became a coherent whole that could be put into words (Namer 1987, 140–57). Something similar seems to be occurring in Latin American, African, and Asian Bible movements. Fragmented experiences of oppression and disappearances have become a coherent collective memory. This type of memory is called visceral memory. In the small Bible reading groups, a similar process of "remembering" has also, in my view, been set in motion.

Visceral memory has to do with why a certain event or person means so much to us and proves to be determinative for our corporate existence (Irwin-Zarecka 1994). Visceral memories are memories of profound suffering, of innocent people who have been afflicted by evil: the bishop who was killed for his prophetic indictment, or the loved one who disappeared because he or she asked why the poor have no bread. It is the memory of suffering—suffering that overcomes people and can be explained by nothing other than pure human wickedness—that makes

---

3. Semeia Studies 52 is devoted entirely to this topic.

people furious and speechless and that is constitutive for the community that has made the sacrifices.

Many traces of visceral memories can be found in our empirical material: traces of age-old suffering, poverty, and exclusion caused by colonialism, apartheid, the caste system, the exclusion of women—and the list goes on.

"Without culture we are dead," an Aymara participant from Bolivia said.

> The Aymaras have a splendid culture. . . . There is always a duality; every person has part of a man and part of a woman in him or her. The conquest by the Spanish soldiers changed our culture. If that had not happened, then our culture would have been friendly and beautiful. . . .

A Brazilian group reported that a particular event in the life of the group had occurred in 1999—when the group had come together four years prior. The group members had remembered the 500-year anniversary of the occupation of Latin America: "These were times of reflection and fraternization *[foram momentos de reflexão e confraternização]*."

A Colombian group said, "One of the problems that we are wrestling with is the fact that many families live in crowded conditions: two or three families have to live in a small house, and a whole family lives in one room. The people have no access to social security, education, and health."

The visceral memories of groups from India speak of the unimaginable suffering that the caste system has caused. A group of casteless participants said:

> In most of the villages and hamlets in our country, India, we find the colonies of the downtrodden to be the borders (or) ending area of the village. In some cases this is far away from the main village. Some of the colonies are adjacent to the graveyards. It can easily be concluded that these colonies are forced to be located and constructed such that these places will under no circumstance be a touching point to the top group. In case there is a situation where the privileged people have to pass along the road of the Dalits, these unfortunate people have to walk down the road and regard them. Nevertheless, Dalit women should remain indoors.

In a Korean reading report, as in many other reading reports, a basic element of the social memory is the exclusion of women:

> I feel so small under the present church structure because women have no proper position within the church. Church members have a bias about women ministers in that they think women are inferior to men. They do not want to have women as their leaders but as their servants.

In South African groups, the race question and experience of apartheid are elements that cannot be erased from memory. A group of white participants wrote:

> The majority of the members are admitting their role in the sad past of the country, and are dedicated to contributing to the future of the country with all its peoples.

The reporter for a group of Xhosa participants wrote:

> The angle from which the text was approached was introduced by the first speaker. He introduced the issue of racism as an issue in the text as well and as a problem current in the community.

Discrimination also played a fundamental role in the memory of a group of Mexican immigrants in the US:

> Immigrant families struggle to feel at home in a foreign context, raising their children in English-speaking schools, surrounded by the dominant white culture. Many immigrants complain of being discriminated against.

A final example is from El Salvador. The visceral memories of the group are profoundly marked by the question of impunity *(impunidad)*. The story in Luke 18 of the woman who appeals in vain to the judge is also read from this perspective:

> This widow does the same as we do when we ask that justice be done to us for our sons who have been killed and lie dispersed throughout these hills and of whom the judges know nothing.

These examples will suffice. What I want to show with these examples is that the joint reading of Bible texts can be a catalyst for the articulation of visceral memories (Aalbersberg–van Loon 2003). That this happens lies in the encounter between one's own life story and the Bible text; the discussion on the text mobilizes the visceral memories of the group. What has lain hidden and enclosed in the memory—unarticulated, for there were no words for it and there was no one listening—is now mobilized by the Bible text in the safe space of the small group.[4]

---

4. In this connection see also the following remarks by Catherine Kohler Riessman: "Despite the seeming universality of the discourse form, some experiences are extremely difficult to speak about. Political conditions constrain particular events from being narrated. The ordinary response to atrocities is to banish them from awareness. Survivors of political torture, war, and sexual crimes silence themselves and are silenced because it is too difficult to tell and to listen. Rape survivors, for example, may not be able to talk about what they experienced as terrorizing violations because others do not regard them as violations. Under these circumstances, women may have difficulty even naming their experience. If it is spoken about, the experience emerges as a kind of 'prenarrative': it does not develop or progress in time, and it does not reveal the storyteller's feelings or interpretations of events". Social movements aid individuals to name their injuries, connect with others, and engage in political action. Research interviewers can also bear witness" (Kohler Riessman 2002, 220).

If I underscore the healing power of the encounter between one's own visceral memories and the Bible text, I am then connecting with the experience of Latin American and African biblical theologians. Since the 1980s, biblical scholars in these areas as well as elsewhere have been deeply moved by the *lectura popular de la Biblia*—what the poor do with Bible texts. The Bible becomes a new book in the hands of the poor. The old patristic adage that the Bible is *liber et speculum*, book and mirror, is found often in the literature: that is how the contemporary poor read the Bible. Pablo Richard's often quoted statement that the whole Bible was made by the poor and contains the *memoria histórica*, the social memory, of the poor refers to the special alliance between people and the Bible (Richard 1982, 1984). However much this sweeping statement can be criticized (de Wit 2006b), its importance is that it refers to the character of the encounter between Bible texts and the poor, and that people are thus sensitive to the Scriptures containing far more visceral memories than traditional biblical scholarship has thought.[5]

The Processing of Trauma. Another element emerges from the foregoing paragraph that emphasizes the value of joint Bible reading—namely, that it can contribute to the processing of trauma. I maintain that what is true for all contextual theologies—that an important element of these schemes is the processing of trauma[6] (an analytical perspective that is much too absent from Western approaches)—also holds true for contextual Bible reading. In the examples given above of visceral memories, trauma is almost always present. The empirical material contains many references to the processing of trauma. Here are some examples.

In John 4:20, the Samaritan woman asks whether God can be worshiped only in the temple. This is an immense problem for Dalit women in India, who are not allowed into the temple. "Why does the woman suddenly begin talking about worship?" someone from these untouchables asked. "The Samaritan woman did not fit into the existing forms of worship," another answered, "maybe because she, as an outcast, was not allowed in." "But," another woman answered, "where people who are in pain are excluded, God cannot be found either. God cannot be where there is no place for us!"

A Bolivian women's group wrote:

> The objective of the gatherings is to share God's word and to share needs and personal problems, helping one another.

---

5. What, for example, is one to think of a rereading of the resurrection narrative as a bearer of social memory and as a form of trauma processing by the disciples of Jesus of Nazareth?

6. One can think of a number of the following specific characteristics of liberation theologies, Dalit theology, Minjung theology, black theology, feminist theology, etc.: great creativity, specifying the images of the enemy and the accompanying construction of a new self-image, certainty about how the world works, emphasis on the gratuity principle, a new spirituality and liturgical forms, a new view of core symbols of Christianity, an entirely new understanding of Bible texts, emphasis on the importance of "remembering" and the reenactment of atrocities, the formation of communities (basic communities), the importance of praxis.

> Among the group, they help and encourage when their members are not good spiritually, physically, and morally speaking.

A Brazilian group reported:

> The resistance of our people in their perpetual struggle to survive is strong, whereby people search for forms that can quench our thirst for better times. Religion is an important element in this resistance. And even if religion is used to justify the existing situation, religion will be used by a not insignificant part of the people as a form of relief, of strengthening solidarity, of becoming conscious in the search for the transformation of this reality.

Here is another example from the Philippines. A Filipino group of ex-prostitutes read the story of the Samaritan woman together with a Dutch group. A discussion arose on the identity of the Samaritan woman and what she had done. The Dutch group saw her as a feminist: she asked questions, and she did not do what Jesus asked. The Filipino group was convinced that the Samaritan woman was a prostitute. They said:

> We know what that is. If you have been a prostitute, you never want to speak about the experience. And you see that also in Jesus' reaction. For Jesus heals her! He asks one question about her husbands; she says one sentence—I have no husband—and then Jesus fills in the rest of her story. She does not have to tell it; perhaps she is not able to. Jesus' actions are therapeutic; they are the processing of trauma.

I will give one last example through a photo. For a group from Colombia that read the text of Luke 18 together with other groups on the continent, reading the

New text generated by a Colombian group, indicating that communal Bible reading can be a place where people process trauma.

Bible text generated an entirely new text, full of the memory of and longing for justice. The text on the page was put in the form of the body of someone who had been murdered and read:

> Half a year ago four boys were murdered at a bus stop. One of them was Juan Carlos. He was wounded very seriously by the bullets and died three days later in the hospital at nine-thirty in the morning. People began talking immediately about "social cleansing" *(limpieza social)* and accused the four of being thieves. Up to the present there has been no justice in connection with these four murders, and nothing is known.

The examples allow one to draw the conclusion that communal Bible reading can be a place where people process trauma. But we can go one step further. Joint Bible reading appears to contribute to posttraumatic growth, an important dimension of which is a new spirituality. Behavioral psychology and the psychology of religion have been aware for a long time that trauma not only can lead to pathological behavior, but can also contribute to the renewal of one's self-image, to another worldview, and to more empathy and sensitivity. The lists of characteristics of posttraumatic growth are extensive,[7] and some of these basic characteristics also can be found in the reading reports. They have to do primarily with spirituality, with a social space in which memories and experiences can be shared, and with the power of *relectura*—that is, the possibility of reading the original source texts of the religious tradition from a new perspective. I will provide a few examples.

"I feel that in moments of pain, when reading the Bible, I find hope, and some options that generate life," said an Aymara participant in a Bolivian group.

"We are members of three Bible groups of the Mental Health Hospital in M," a German group wrote.[8]

> John 4:6 is important to us. Verse 6—Jesus sat down at the well because he was tired—corresponds to the reality of our lives. We are also often tired and need refreshment. One must believe in oneself, otherwise everything is lost. . . . The well is a place where one goes to quench one's thirst. Where is our

---

7. Ruard Ganzevoort lists a number of characteristics of posttraumatic growth that we frequently encounter in our empirical material. "The recognition and management of uncertainty, the integration of affect and cognition, and the recognition and acceptance of human limitation; increased empathy, compassion and connectedness; appreciation of the value and frailty of life, appreciation of new possibilities." Very important are "social support, and communal motives in identity-construction." Spiritual growth is strengthened by the "the offering of hope and encouragement, the satisfaction of important personal needs, and the relationship with others." See Ganzevoort 2005, 344–61.

8. This Mental Health Hospital offers facilities for people who have committed crimes and were ordered by the court to undergo therapy. On average, people must stay about six years; some remain longer than ten years. Therefore, the search for a hope-filled future is one of the most important questions in life. This group has great interest in contacts with people who read the Bible outside the Mental Health Hospital.

"well"? The place where we are encouraged to live perhaps! This can be the Bible Group.

In Colombia, a conflict zone, the story of the widow and the judge in Luke 18 was read: "The text shows that the widow stubbornly keeps pushing the judge until the judge helps her. That teaches us not to lose heart for what we want to achieve."

A Salvadoran women's group that also read Luke 18 was asked with whom they identified. The women were reading the text together with the other Latin American groups mentioned above. All of them were victims of *impunidad*—the fact that the most horrific crimes remain unpunished. "With the widow, for she does not rest until justice is done . . . exactly like our committee [for human rights], which everyone says should now stop. . . . But no justice has been done yet! How can we stop?"

An Argentinian group that read John 4 said, "What we are doing here nourishes our hope—making the decision to want to be God's instrument and to get going."

These examples will suffice. We lack the space here to look further at the relationship between joint Bible reading and the processing of trauma. I hope that I have made it plausible that there is a relationship here and also how fruitful this form of Bible reading can be for healing.

7

On Board

I have attempted above to show the value of communal Bible reading. But is there a surplus value when it happens in intercultural perspective? How do ordinary readers escape what Bakhtin has called dominant reading traditions?[1] In short, how do ordinary readers do strange things with Bible texts if they are on board a boat with other readers?

Motivation

Cultural studies refer to a whole cluster of conditions necessary for the thawing of positions, for growth, and for the development of intercultural competence. They are grouped together under categories of knowledge, skills, and motivation. One of the most important is having the right motivation. People distinguish between three kinds of motivation, which we have mentioned already. The most fruitful for growth is the motivation for validity—the willingness to be challenged, or, following Procee, the willingness to interact—the result of which leaves traces in the self.

In our empirical material, a significant correlation between this type of motivation and growth emerged, as did the fact that the overwhelming majority of participants was entering the discussion with the willingness to be challenged. The participants did not want to meet exotic groups from a different world and leave it at that; they wanted to learn and change. The list of terms they used to describe their hopes for the interactions was long. They spoke expectantly of "mutual learning," "learning about the world from another," "dialogue as a new form of discussing faith," "sharing life's experiences," and "wanting to go to the

---

1. Marianne Paas gives a nice example from a Dutch group: "Everyone already had his or her own conceptions about this story. It is noticeable in the group that the conceptions that are connected with the traditional history of exegesis sometimes clash with a desire to look differently at the story. . . . We exchanged our conceptions and feelings. . . . But there did not seem to be much movement here. The conceptions that we already had with this story seem to be quite fixed" (Paas 2004, 90).

source together." From the long list of examples, I will share three that represent the motivation of the majority of participants.

A participant from the US formulated his motivation as follows:

> I will gain a deeper perspective by looking at other people's way of interpreting the Bible from many different cultural and economic backgrounds or social statuses. I hope that it would definitely have a positive effect on my faith journey. I hope that it would not be just "neat" or "cool" or something that just tickles my brain. I am really searching for a change in my own life, a real change. I desire to somehow connect Scripture study with real life. That is what I hope for during this and all of the studies that we do together.

The reporter for a Scottish group wrote about the group's motivation:

> The group all agreed to come together for this project and to read John 4 with open minds and a willingness to learn from and be challenged by each other's contribution and mutual participation. We also recognise that there are many aspects of learning and knowledge other than our own. We look forward to broadening our understanding of our common humanity through engaging with the project reading of John 4.

A "little old lady" from the US revealed:

> My background is Presbyterian and . . . my heart longs to bring people into a Bible study. When you do a Bible study, you are the one who is enriched, and I have done two. I have done Ephesians, and last year I did Jeremiah. And the growth was within myself. I was excited to hear other people talk about what it meant to them, but my perspective is that of a white little old lady in orthopedic shoes . . . and I want to change that.

Scriptural Attitude

Not all readers of religious texts want to go on board with other readers. But if they do, they are nourished by a certain attitude. With Wilfred Cantwell Smith, I call this "a scriptural attitude" and consider it to be a quality of Scripture itself. I consider this scriptural attitude to be an answer to the almost incomprehensible combination of elements that makes a collection of historical texts Scripture. This combination is responsible for the fact that a discussion of a Bible text truly has a different status and content than a discussion of a secular text.

In his study of the importance of sacred texts in religions, *What is Scripture?*, Smith reassesses the concept of Scripture. Scripture is not merely a book or a collection of books having an exceptional status within a religious system, Smith says, but a human activity in the first place (Smith 1993). Scriptural attitude is thus a response to Scripture. Here, it concerns an attitude of respect—the feeling of standing on sacred ground. This is the attitude we have continually encountered in our empirical material. It has been overwhelming to see hundreds of readers across the world bowed over the texts in deep respect.

What makes the Bible special and invites a special response is not only its status; the narrative character and literary form of its texts; and its combination of the religious, the fictional, and the historical.[2] No, it is more. It also has to do with its development. Scripture has grown, and many texts are the products of small communities; one sees the fingerprints of the disenfranchised and excluded. The Bible is a democratic product; it contains different points of view. It is also the result of having been continuously understood in conjunction with different cultures and in confrontation with colonial powers, with empire. The interaction between what Fishbane has called the *traditum* (the transmitted text) and the *traditio* (the transmission dynamics, of making the text relevant to today) is to a large degree determinative for the content of the texts (Fishbane 1985). It can be said that the development of the canon prepared a ready model for an attitude of a responsible answer to the texts. Having a scriptural attitude means reading as if one were walking on sacred ground—not as a conqueror in full marching kit, but carefully, gropingly, with shoes removed. This is ground on which the other is welcome, for the simple reason that it is not one's own but belongs to an Other.

In looking at Scripture interculturally, we are attempting to be responsible for what Scripture is and to lead participants to a scriptural attitude. This attitude is found among a great many participants.

Strange Things . . .

From the perspective of petrified faith traditions and fundamentalistic forms of readings, which are geared toward retaining power, one can say that readers who get on board the boat with very different readers do extremely strange things. They welcome the other as an epiphanic space. They write letters to complete strangers, send pictures, and invite them to visit. They remove their masks and admire or criticize one another. They make themselves vulnerable and jump for joy when they receive a response from the partner group. They discover not only strange worlds but also great commonalities. They break through loneliness and sometimes comfort one another.

This space is one within which a new spirituality takes shape. Prejudices are adjusted, the situation of asymmetry is involved critically in the discussion, and the powerless and the powerful are recognized as equals. Readers attempt to discover origins of and structure in the differences, relativizing them and searching for what gives life. They look critically at their own context. They criticize mechanisms of exclusion in the partner group and begin to notice their own as well.

---

2   "Bible stories combine the power of the religious, the fictional, and the historical," Edwin Koster writes. "The figurative language of narratives is able to transcend finite reality and can bring up the presupposed transcendent dimension of reality" (Koster 2005, 294).

A lot also happens hermeneutically. The reading of the Bible text takes the form of a discussion, and faith takes the form of a search. There is a reorientation to one's own interpretation, a broadening of horizons. People discover their own blind spots—the power and sometimes paralysis of their dominant reading tradition.

In short, intercultural Bible reading brings a great deal of good to the surface in people. Here appears, at a micro level and sometimes very briefly, what Schreiter describes as the contours of a new catholicity:

> A new catholicity, then, is marked by a wholeness of inclusion and fullness of faith in a pattern of intercultural exchange and communication. To the extent that this catholicity can be realized, it may provide a paradigm for what a universal theology might look like today, able to encompass both sameness and difference, rooted in an orthopraxis providing *teloi* for a globalized society. (Schreiter 1997, 133)

A Small Gesture of Love

There is still one intriguing question to answer. I hope that I have made clear that a great deal happens in the intercultural encounter, but how is that to be understood in terms of the relationship between interpretation and praxis? This has been much discussed in contextual theologies. The Argentinian biblical theologian José Severino Croatto calls reflection on this relationship one of the main tasks of Latin American hermeneutics and considers the praxis of the contemporary interpreter to be the fundamental orientation point of the understanding of the text. Severino wonders: How can the text become a message for praxis and the praxis a message for the understanding of the text?[3]

The question is complex and challenging. Much depends on how praxis is defined. In the early years of liberation theology and the rise of the so-called Bible movement in Latin America, praxis became defined primarily in a sociopolitical way: "The Psalms in the Struggle of the People," "The Bible in the Liberation of the People," "The Bible, the *Frente*, and the Revolution," to mention a few examples of articles published in those years (de Wit 1991, 42ff.). And a still very popular hermeneutical scheme in Latin America is the trio *ver, juzgar, actuar* (seeing, judging, acting), which indicates how the relationship with praxis was discussed in a carefree way and how close the relationship between reading, interpretation, and action was thought to be. The following statement from a Mexican

---

3. "En vez de considerar el texto como un residuo del pasado, una hermenéutica latinoamericana de liberación deberá encontrar una nueva respuesta a la pregunta cómo las coordenadas texto y praxis actual pueden ser relacionadas de tal manera que el texto bíblico puede ser mensaje para la praxis y la actual praxis para la comprensión del texto bíblico. Esta es la tarea de la nueva hermenéutica latinoamericana." (How can the coordinates of praxis and text be brought into connection with each other in such a way that the Bible text is a message for the praxis and the current praxis a message for the text?) On this see also Severino Croatto 1994; de Wit 1991.

reading community is an example of what people constantly encountered in the 1980s:

> In the basic church communities we reflect on the Word of God on the basis of our concrete reality. We change that reality by the power of the Word. . . . All of this has been a long learning process in which we learned to listen to the Word of God *from the perspective of the practice of liberation* (de Wit 1991, 44; my italics).

The start of the problem that I am now talking about becomes visible when one pays close attention to the use of the word *praxis*. Arthur McGovern already demonstrated in the 1990s that the concept of praxis had a wide spectrum of meanings in liberation theology as a whole but also among individual writers such as Gustavo Gutiérrez (McGovern 1990, 32ff.; van Nieuwenhove 1991). I discovered that this was also true of Severino Croatto (de Wit 1991, 210ff., 288ff.). For them, praxis extends from unselfish love up to and including sociopolitical revolutionary praxis that is intended to change society. Thus, we do not get very far with heavily accentuated statements about the correlation between Bible reading and praxis. Of course, Bible texts are carried on placards in protest marches and used in all kinds of ways, but the relationship is unclear. For example, it is unclear whether the praxis of liberation is a product of the new, careful way of Bible reading, or whether the text is already held hostage by an existing praxis.[4] There is no analysis of how the relationship works. Fortunately, liberation theologians have become quite a bit more modest in recent years in their claims and have discovered the importance of *cotidianidad* (the everyday) as sacramental space. In his very last publication, José Míguez Bonino pointed to the reorientation of hope and to the importance of dialogue and small gestures (Míguez Bonino 2004, 42–43).

I come to my point. What do we see if we look at the empirical material in terms of praxeological effect? If we use the sociopolitical praxis concept found in liberation theology, we actually see very little. In 3,000 pages of empirical material, only one example can be found of a group that goes directly into action after reading a text: a group of Ghanaian men who want to assemble a committee against polygamy. Further, in liberation theology we do not see evidence of a one-to-one relationship between reading and praxis; we see a great deal on the level of "We should . . . ," "We will now . . . ," "We had to . . . ," "We will soon . . ."

What lessons does our research then yield with respect to the relationship between reading Bible texts and their effect? I see the following.

In the first place, it shows that sacred texts do not need to be considered as an object or as the barrel of a gun directed at others. They can be meeting places where people search together for peace, salvation, and change. This fundamen-

---

4. "You read what you are ready for; in other words, add something to what was already actually present in embryonic form" (Vanheste 1981, 193).

tal observation immediately relativizes all one-sided language about the relation between sacred texts and terror and prompts further research.

In the second place, the material shows that the relationship between read-ers' interpretation and their dominant reading tradition is extraordinarily close. A dominant tradition can either overrule readers' social status or political affinity or make it operational. For example, an Argentinean basic Christian community group read John 4 entirely in terms of the *ver-juzgar-actuar* scheme mentioned above, in which *actuar*—action—was not given any content. At the same time, a Nicaraguan Pentecostal group read John 4 entirely in terms of the sin-repentance-salvation scheme, without any reference to the perplexing political and social situation in Nicaragua at that time.

The implication of this observation is that, if the power of dominant reading traditions is such that they can influence deeply a process of understanding and that two groups that read the same text at the same time come to very differ-ent conclusions, the text is, in fact, the great absent figure here. In other words, if images from texts in the Bible or the Qur'an are accompanied immediately by images of human actions (e.g., of terror and destruction), thus suggesting an immediate connection between both practices, then the relationship between text and practice is represented in an inadequate and irresponsible manner, and the suggested intimate connection between reading and acting is nonexistent. The re-lationship between sacred texts and human action is simplified in a very suggestive and improper way. What is in fact much more complex than the images reveal is reduced to a one-to-one relationship.

In this type of process, the text becomes simply a lackey of the user's exist-ing convictions. Can texts be condemned purely on the basis of bad users? If one wants to condemn users of texts from Holy Books, then one should look first at the users' dominant reading tradition—and at the whole of the norms and values that orients it—rather than at the text. There are, after all, other readers of the same texts who come to an entirely different praxis.

Dominant reading traditions derive their power from the social domain in which they are operative and which they legitimize. They are like blocks of ice to which people are frozen because they cannot or do not want to leave the social domain. Readers who want to be responsible for the text not only for themselves but also for other and future readers must sometimes be extracted from the dominant reading tradition. Confrontation is then necessary, but—as we already said—it must be organized, for the most part. That is exactly the intention behind intercultural Bible reading. The interaction between the Argentinean and the Nicaraguan groups yields a spectacular change.

The third lesson of our research is that to develop another view of liberation, one must think small and simply about liberation. A great deal happens—also much that is liberating—when people read the Bible together, but it is mostly on a level other than the metalevel of politics. This effect escapes us if we do not think otherwise about liberation. The empirical material asks us to see the small gesture, the hand that is ready, as a liberation praxis—the small gesture that is the beginning of something new, whose end is unknown. The practice that we want to foster is modest and simple. It is located in the sphere of the transformation of thinking and feeling, of what the Bible calls "conversion": first liberation *to* and then liberation *from*. It is a sequence of small movements: First, in the encounter with the elsewhere and otherwise of the other, there is the emptying, the distance from power, the vulnerability. Then there is an alliance or, as one participant called it, the "small bond of friendship." Next, there is discussion of the asymmetry to which the liberation of the other becomes a message. And then—perhaps sometime, who knows when?—change in society occurs.

From a small gesture of love to something else—is that not in fact the central theme of the story of the encounter between Jesus and the Samaritan woman at the well? Salvation comes to us from outside ourselves. It is an encounter that leads to radical changes but begins with a small, simple gesture, "Will you give me a drink?"

The final lesson is this. The empirical material is unimaginably rich and varied. But does it not lead to a hermeneutical impotence of sorts? Is the text still given a chance to speak? Is something still shared in the intercultural practice of reading? The answer must be that diversity and polysemy of texts are not the same as paralysis and indifference. It is precisely the diversity that makes the text a gift for many. The diversity of ethical answers to the text is a tribute to its ability to orient different communities in different ways. Levinas expresses this concept as follows:

> The irreducible multiplicity of readings is a reflection of lived ethics. Multiplicity or plurivocity is not a flaw, but a product of and tribute to that lived ethics. What constitutes the fundamental truth of meaning, then, is not a common denominator, which would be reductive, but a unique service, the singularity of each one in the face of the other.

All of the reading groups discovered that victory lies in the encounter and that the text cracks dominant cultural, social, political, and religious codes in a radical and absolutely revelatory way. Everything comes up in John 4: ethnicity, gender, exclusion, status, social difference, tradition, making tradition relevant to the present, sacred places, the teacher, his students. This variety also points to the varied nature of liberation, which can be worked out in each faith community's particular situation in its own way—as a unique service of the text to the unique community. The community of the Indian Dalit women is unique, as is its partner group in the Netherlands. The group of Korean students is unique, as is its partner group in Colombia. Intercultural discussions of faith will always be directed at the liberation of the other, beyond one's own liberation.[5] What brings about one's

---

5. By regauging and nuancing the concept of liberation, I am attempting to find an answer to the protests that come immediately from hermeneutics that want to read "with" the poor as soon as otherness is welcomed. It will immediately be asked: Where does this emphasis on otherness, dialogue and diversity come from? People will quickly see the welcoming of otherness as a betrayal of the liberation project. What if the other is the oppressor? With this question on his tongue, Ricoeur asks Levinas: How do we distinguish the "master from the executioner, the master who calls for a disciple from the master who requires a slave"? Is the emphasis on the importance of otherness not a veiled neocolonial appeal to the

own liberation does not automatically include that which brings about liberation for the other. It is precisely the discussion with the other that leads people to insights into the plurality and diversity of ethical answers, liberating them from obsession with their own liberation and sensitizing them to the fact that the text wants to provide a unique service to each reader.

Plurality thus results from having different answers to a text. These answers can converge into an identical answer to difference—namely, peace. We see this answer portrayed as a symbolic expression that summarizes the interaction between two unique groups, one in Hungary and one in the Netherlands, in the following photograph.

Dove with "justice, light for the world, love" in Dutch and Hungarian, summarizing the interaction between two partner groups.

---

victims of the rich and the conquistadores in this world to welcome these rich and conquistadores as friends in the end?

8

The Crocodile Lives in the Water, and Yet He Breathes Air

Intercultural hermeneutics is aimed at interaction. But Bible texts are not only meeting places for ordinary readers; they also are visited intensively by professional readers with their own expertise and interests. Professional readers are responsible for contributing to unfolding the meanings that the text could have had in its historical setting. How can there be adequate reflection on their involvement with what ordinary readers do with texts? Before we formulate an answer, it must be stated that attempting to capture contemporary Western exegesis in one definition—something non-Western exegetes sometimes do—seldom amounts to more than reduction and trivialization. The diversity of "Western" methods of exegesis that are used in abundance outside the West is also great. But to make these observations is not to deny that there are dominant reading traditions in the West.

What can the meaning be of contact between, for example, readings of John 4 by Rudolf Bultmann and by a divorced Ghanaian mother of eight children? From the perspective of exegesis, for professional readers to interact with ordinary readers, they must be willing to be involved in some way in the processes of appropriation and in the effect of the text. We have stated already that much has been written on the latter, especially by biblical scholars in the Southern Hemisphere; in their context, it is an urgent matter to evoke a word of salvation from Scripture in situations of obvious suffering and premature death. Many exegetes in the Southern Hemisphere argue that people who are as intensively involved with the text as professional Bible readers are must be willing to take responsibility for the text as message. This topic was discussed for fifty numbers in the journal *Revista de Interpretación Bíblica Latinoamericana* (*RIBLA*): How can the exegete read and explain Bible texts in such a way that they become a message of liberation, salvation, and space for contemporary ordinary readers—who are often the poor? It is a central goal of all genitive hermeneutics. That some exegetes are unwilling to cooperate in this work is incomprehensible for these biblical scholars in the Southern Hemisphere.

Although I am aware of the pitfalls that await the socially engaged exegete (de Wit 1991; 2008), I do agree with many of my colleagues from the South. What self-respecting biblical theologian would not want to go where his or her primary object has a healing effect? I do not see why professional readers would not want to go on board with ordinary readers—more than once in a while—to do strange, but at the same time (viewed exegetically) extraordinarily relevant things with texts. A Ghanaian proverb states, "The crocodile lives in the water, and yet he breathes air." That is what exegetes should want to be able to do.

I have some arguments to support this claim. How exegetes deal with texts can have advantages with respect to the sometimes narcissistic behavior of ordinary readers. Without becoming arbiters of meaning,[1] exegetes can expose the dangerous pathological characteristics of appropriation. Second, why should exegetes leave the fascinating area of *relectura* to others? The involvement of contemporary reception criticism and intercultural hermeneutics in a discipline that is quickly declining in popularity would be good for it. Then there is, again, an ethical argument: if exegesis is striving for completeness and not to reduce the texts' transcendence, it cannot exclude the overwhelmingly large group of ordinary readers, for their experiences with the text will mean something for the text. The task of the exegete is then to make these experiences fruitful for the text, making it capable of unfolding its meaning potential.

But these arguments do not answer another question, which can be formulated in the following way, with a variation on the well-known statement by Von Rad: How can an exegete who intends to establish the meaning of the text in terms of an academically supported minimum participate in the space where the text unfolds maximally as message, as kerygma? That brings me to a methodological question.

Methodological Ludism and Hermeneutics

I believe that the problem confronting us here is a hermeneutical variant of the problem for which methodological ludism in anthropology wants to offer a solution.[2] With the insights of this theory, I will attempt to construct a bridge between spontaneous reading and a systematic, critical approach to the text.

The problem for which anthropologists seek a solution via methodological ludism is that of the relationship between practitioners of a religion and the science that studies religion. "Those doing religious studies and believers are not pleasant bedfellows," Droogers writes (2006). Academics do not accept religious views of science, and believers are shocked by what scientists say about religion.

---

1. A problem that plays an immense role in genitive hermeneutics. See my dissertation on the relationship between relevance and pertinence in biblical studies (de Wit 1991).

2. For the following I am drawing on the many publications by André Droogers on methodological ludism. Methodological ludism is defined as follows: "The capacity to deal simultaneously and subjunctively with two or more ways of classifying reality." For this and what follows see Droogers 2006, where other literature also can be found.

Scientists who investigate religion usually are either atheists or agnostics methodologically: they refrain from making judgments as to the "truth" of a religion and religious practices. The believer reproaches the scientist with the statement that one can observe as much as one wishes, but as long as the observer him/herself does not participate in the search for transcendence, the investigation will continue to have a hole and will always be deficient. One can state, and one can analyze, but the experience of transcendence, of faith, will remain out of reach. The problem is related to the opposition between emic and etic—roughly, the perspective of "insiders" and "academic outsiders." What methodological ludism asks from the scholar in religious studies in that she work on the interface between observation and surrender.

The hermeneutical parallel can be formulated as follows. Tension exists between ordinary readers of biblical texts and those who analyze the texts. Professional readers accept neither religious views of exegesis nor views of its meaning from the perspective of the effect of the text. Since Spinoza, professional readers have viewed appropriation processes with suspicion. On the other hand, readers who believe are often shocked by the detachment of academic readers and the results of academic research. They are shocked in two ways: in their views of faith and in academics' unwillingness to include in their research that which is essential for ordinary readers. Professional Bible readers are, viewed technically, usually atheists or agnostics methodologically: they refrain from making judgments as to the "truth" of the text and its effect. They are accused of never understanding the actual depth of a text. They will never understand how a text works because they do not participate—because of their discipline's epistemological rules, they are unable to—in what is essential for the overwhelming majority of people who read the Bible—namely, its effect. In the view of ordinary Bible readers, exegesis all too often plays the role of umpire, whereas it is, of course, merely one of the players—with its own rules and results.

Methodological ludism attempts to find a way out via the notion of play, which also plays an important role in hermeneutics. Gadamer underscores the character of all understanding as play. Understanding is for the translator what a match is for a sportsman or sportswoman: it is play. In Gadamer, play has a few fundamental connotations: it does not represent freedom or noncommitment as in some later postmodern hermeneutical schemes. In Gadamer, play is not something one does in one's free time but a way of looking at how people handle things, reality or texts. It is a critical, deconstructive concept, for it humiliates power. Play breaks through the view that a subject-object relationship exists between reader and text; play sees that relationship as an event. Something happens between the text and the reader: both participate in the game, and the game affects both. The notion of play relativizes approaches to the text that claim that they alone are valid, for it points to other approaches that play by different rules with different results (Gadamer 1986, 301ff.; 1990, 108ff.).

Exegesis values its academic status highly. But a brief look at the results of exegetical research suffices to underscore its character as play. As long as two scholars can differ by as much as a thousand years on the question of when the book Judges was written, some will view the book as a story of chaos and extreme violence, and others will view it as a kind of utopian sociopolitical project (de Wit 2000; 2001, 71–96). As long as biblical studies lack consensus on most topics and its methods continue to expand, there is no reason to consider only the popular reading of the Bible as play. Exegesis is also play.

I believe that the tension between popular reading of the Bible and exegesis can be overcome—even rendered fruitful—if we view both exegesis and the spontaneous understanding from the perspective of play. Methodological ludism in the hermeneutical sense can then be defined as the ability to deal successively with radically different ways in which a Bible text's meaning is construed, to understand which rules people use, and to analyze how these rules can complement each other. Methodological ludism in hermeneutics also can become operational through the recognition of the limitations of the rules of play of methodological atheism or agnosticism.

The heart of the matter here is that the rules for working with the text as a historical object are very different from those for living in the text and seeing it as ally, as traveling companion. When people see the effect that Bible texts can have on people in situations of conflict, persecution, and deep suffering—the meanings that Bible texts receive when people carry them in protest marches, sing them in front of court buildings, mutter them in morgues where they seek the bodies of those who have been kidnapped and tortured, and recite them on African fields to gain fertility, healing, and success—they then will realize that the effect is an element that can never be understood from a distance, yet it can be of surprising exegetical importance. Methodological ludism challenges the rules of play of methodological atheism and agnosticism, asking which rules in that epistemological charter, or in the culture or context they want to serve, prevent exegetes from becoming insiders rather than outsiders and from listening carefully where the text has its effect. It asks whether it is possible that the rules of play could be "creolized." On the other hand, play and the rules of appropriation processes—the "creolization" of the text in making it relevant to the present—also are studied.

The place of methodological ludism is thus indeed the boat, the Third Bank of the River, where the exegete has gone on board with the spontaneous reader. The application of the concept of play in the area of competitive paradigms can mean that power mechanisms are relativized and reductionism becomes manifest. Methodological ludism in hermeneutical perspective attempts to connect elements that are contradictory, conflicting, and different; the concept of play is intended to make this confrontation fruitful. Whoever sees the relationship between spontaneous understanding and exegesis not as hierarchical but as complementary understands that here, at the interface between observation and surrender, there can be a double gift—a gift to both sides of the river. The practice of the professional readers is enriched by the gift from the bearers of the text's effect as a message for the text. The gift for ordinary readers is that their appropriation-oriented reading strategies are taken seriously and presented to the text as an exegetical question.

On the Third Bank of the River

From the hundreds of examples in our empirical material that make clear the importance of being on the Third Bank of the River, I will give only a few. While I am deeply convinced of the importance of exegesis for spontaneous understanding of the text, I am addressing the ordinary reader here and therefore will attempt to show the importance of reading strategies for exegesis. What positive things can happen on board when ordinary and professional readers sit across from each other?

We already discussed the story of the widow and the judge in Luke 18, a sober story of not more than a few verses. Groups from Peru, Colombia, El Salvador, and Guatemala read this story at the same time and subsequently discussed it with one another.[3] Many visceral memories came to the surface for these reading groups, expanding the number of reading possibilities of the story. These possibilities are extraordinarily relevant for homiletics and also hold special importance for exegesis.

The story reminded some people in Peru of the time they were chased away from the market where they had had a stall for years, because others had bought the land. The church did nothing. Someone else from the group thought of a mother whose child who was infected with HIV via a blood transfusion because the nurses made a mistake. The hospital refused to take responsibility for the child. Another woman thought of the family members of victims of political violence. "The text does not go into detail, but for us is full of experiences that touch us in the depths of our being and our deepest experiences," they wrote.

In El Salvador someone said:

> This text is very difficult for me. It does not seem that short when you hear it, for someone who insists so much is full of grief that no one treats her justly. I do not know what happened precisely, but I do know that she is terribly full of pain. Why is this text never read in our churches? I know indeed the story of the crippled woman or the story of the woman with the crumbs, but not this story. When I see how much had to be given to the judge so that she could get some justice, I become terribly angry. Maybe the woman had to bribe him, or who knows what she had to do so that he would give her justice? . . . People have no idea what mothers must do sometimes to receive justice.

In another group in El Salvador, a participant said immediately:

> The text is clear; it is about a woman who asks for justice
> for one of her sons who has fallen in the struggle, and she is
> refused because these cases are dangerous . . . not because they

---

3. A project carried out by the development organization Solidaridad under the supervision of Maria Berends.

are widows but because they will tell, and it is better that they
die than that they begin to tell the terrible things that have
happened.

Finally, another group from Peru found it surprising that the widow continued to go alone, never taking anyone with her, and that nowhere was it stated that
she tried to bribe the judge, which is completely normal in their culture.

What the "third position" yields is that the effect of the story can orient the
exegete with respect to the question if the text fits in the social domain indicated
by the experiences that are relayed. The story of the widow and the judge grows
enormously in significance when its effect is noted. The theological setting as
well—the connection between praying and not giving up, the Father who will
quickly provide justice—receives a new dimension. All kinds of cultural elements
not yet discovered by the exegete herself such as public/private and male/female
roles and dealing with power can appear to be present in the story. Is this story
the bearer of social memory? What can be learned for its translation? Does the
judge yield out of fear that what continually happens to the woman—being hit
in the face—will happen to him? Should the translation then be, ". . . otherwise
I'm going to end up beaten black and blue by her pounding,"[4] "she will attack
me,"[5] "later she will do something to me,"[6] "break my head,"[7] "*para que no venga
continuamente a cansarme,*"[8] "so that she won't eventually wear me out with her
coming!"?[9]

Let us look at a simple example from the interpretations of John 4. In John
4:4, we read, "He had to go through Samaria." Some groups looked very closely at
this verse.

A Dutch group thought it referred to a shortcut: "We think very quickly: it is
the shortest way."

A Indian Dalit women's group felt that what occurs in John 4 is very close
to them—"The sociocultural system in our local ambits is the shadowing of the
fourth chapter of the Gospel according to John!"—and read this verse very differently. For them, it was not a shortcut but Jesus' choice for the poor. "Here, the
villages are the places where the downtrodden can be found," the women said.

> The villages are so situated that 'these places will under no
> circumstance be a touching point to the top group.' But at that
> time our Lord Jesus Christ chose to go to Samaria. . . . Did he
> know that this woman was waiting for him?"

---

4. So the Dutch translations: Lu (Lutherse Vertaling), Lei (Leidsche Vertaling), NBG51 (Nederlands
   Bijbelgenootschap 1951), GNB (Groot Nieuws Bijbel), De Naardense Bijbel.
5. So the Dutch translation NBV (The New Bible Translation).
6. So the Dutch translation Het Boek (The Book).
7. So the Dutch translation SV (Statenvertaling).
8. So the Spanish translation Reina de Valera Actualizada.
9. So the English New International Version.

To me, this contrast seems to be not only a good example of how culture works in interpretation but also something to present to the narrative structure, the cultural codes, and the theology of the text.

I will give a more penetrating example that has to do with the whole narrative and theological structure of John 4. In his fine dissertation, Piet van Veldhuizen shows how until the 1980s, one reading possibility of John 4 did not occur in commentaries and exegesis:[10] the possibility of reading the story as a betrothal type scene story—in other words, John 4 as an engagement story. A type scene is a narrative pattern present in various forms in different stories; John 4 is a variant of the narrative pattern of Genesis 24. Only after 1981, when Robert Alter published his well-known study, *The Art of Biblical Narrative,* did the possible parallel with Genesis 24 appear clear, and biblical scholars began to speak about John 4 as a comic romance, love story, and betrothal story, and about Jesus as lover. Seeing van Veldhuizen's exegesis of John 4 and discovering how fruitful the engagement scene or well story perspective is can end only in sighing: if only Bultmann, Schnackenburg and the many other professional readers who lacked this perspective[11] could have just gotten on board with all of the groups of South African, Dutch, Indian, and Brazilian ordinary readers who had discovered John 4 to be an engagement story at first glance! The empirical material shows that a significant number of groups read the story as having qualities of intimacy, love, betrothal, the erotic, or in any case, a boy-meets-girl atmosphere. I will again give a few examples.

The group from India remarked:

> Places like wells, bore-pumps, are the most possible and appropriate points where a man and a woman can exchange their views and thoughts, if required personally. Generally, these are the public places where love affairs start, and also decisions are made at these places by the love-pairs for their ply, from the kith and kin.

The group quickly added, "These merely are the images of the events during the days of our Lord Jesus Christ. Particularly, when our Lord came to Jacob's well [John 4:6] to meet the Samaritan woman, *but for a holy purpose*" (my italics).

A South African women's group from Kwazulu Natal, South Africa, wrote: "She wants other men to see her and declare love to her; she wants to entice men." Why was she at the well at that time? "She was afraid to meet other women, as they used to gossip about her; she was afraid they would beat her up for enticing

---

10. P. van Veldhuizen 2004, 21–53, gives a historical overview from which I draw. See also the reception criticism research on John 4 by Janeth Norfleete 2002.

11. Van Veldhuizen 2004, 26: "The correspondences between the well narratives as Origen observed them also remained unnoticed in modern biblical scholarship on John 4 for a long time. Only in the 1960s did the fact of these correspondences become mentioned, but the discussion remained mostly on the level of observation, without the conclusions for the interpretation of John 4 being drawn." After 1981 as well there were still many commentaries in which the reference to the Old Testament well stories were lacking; Van Veldhuizen 2004, 33.

their men, because she wanted men to notice her." The facilitator's commentary read:

> In the Zulu tradition the well was a place to fetch water but also served as a social place to meet friends and potential suitors. When a young woman goes to fetch water at an unconventional time, it would be known that she is interested in a man.

The woman is thus looking for a man, but, the group added, what is one to think about Jesus, who is also alone there? Have his disciples gone? "Jesus, they felt, was behaving suspiciously. Perhaps he waited at the well because he wanted to propose love to a woman (given that the well or river was a place for love proposals in their Zulu culture)."

The reporter of the group of transsexuals from India remarked, "The group found that Kannatha [the name the group gave to the Samaritan woman] was unnecessarily talking, probably, complete with flirtatious remarks—maybe to make a new customer out of Jesus!"

From Indonesia: "In one group, the woman was even seen as a prostitute who tried to seduce Jesus or wanted him as her next husband!"

Like many other groups, a Nicaraguan group was surprised that the meeting occurs during the hottest part of the day:

> It was a strange time to be drawing water. It seems as if this woman had a bad name, i.e., she was seen as someone who lived sinfully. It seems that she did not fit within the world of the village. I believe that she was a depraved person: she struck a bargain with any man who came along and had sexual relations with him.

An Indian group wondered what could be discovered in the text if it was read from the perspective of a sex worker:

> The text in John 4:29 talks of the Samaritan woman's willingness to accept that she was a sinner. She is also curious about Jesus' intentions and poses probing questions. Could it be possible that she met all her former lovers at Jacob's well?

A Dutch group discussed the fact that Jesus meets the Samaritan woman at the well at that time alone and speaks to her: "But the servant of Abraham spoke to Rebecca at the well also? *That is the same story*" (my italics).

And perhaps the shortest and nicest response came from a South African group of Pentecostals from the slum Kayelitsha near Capetown: "Believers are the bride of Christ."

I am providing so many examples of the "betrothal" perspective not only to do justice to these ordinary readers and make clear how many groups arrived at this interpretation, but also to show the significance that listening to ordinary readers can have for exegesis. The boy-meets-girl perspective is an extraordinarily powerful one. If the best interpretation is that which does the most justice to most of the text's elements, then it is as if the puzzle falls into place with this perspective. It is determinative for the narrative structure, the dialogues, the cultural components of the story, and not least, the theological orientation of John 4 within the whole of the Gospel.[12] Many elements in John 4 are suddenly given meaning when one reads this story from the perspective of a betrothal type scene: the well, the unusual hour, a man and woman alone, the question of the husbands, the disciples who—as Jesus' family—and the villagers who—as the woman's family—"have to give their permission" for this new relationship. In short, it is a fruitful perspective that is presented to the text from the Third Bank.

If only Bultmann and Schnackenburg had gone on board with a few of the women's groups from Ghana, Colombia, the Netherlands, and the Philippines! The role of the Samaritan woman in the commentaries of these exegetes is completely subordinate; she is an obscure actant who serves only to provide a context for Jesus' actions and self-revelation: "The evangelist had no special interest in the woman." However, if Bultmann and Schnackenburg had considered the perspectives of a number of reading groups on this point, they could have come to a radically different conclusion: the role of the woman *is* crucial. The Indian group saw "He had to go through Samaria" an expression of Jesus' choice for the poor. An American group added, "She is the first woman to whom Jesus can reveal himself. It is as if Jesus can reveal who he is only to her, to this outcast person." (Schnackenburg introduces his commentary on John 4 with the title, "The Self-Revelation of Jesus in Samaria" (1972, 455ff.), forgetting that not only Jesus' mask falls away, but also the woman's.)

A Dutch group remarked, "The Samaritan woman actually helped Jesus to recover who he actually was when she asked how he could ask her to give him some water." A number of groups remarked that it is the woman who pushes the conversation forward; instead of giving Jesus water, she asks a question and keeps on asking. A group in Ghana said, "The story in John 4 of Jesus meeting the Samaritan woman appeared to be an excerpt from the lives of the Ghanaian group." The group asked, "Can a woman just address a man, and is she allowed to do so? Are women in our society not discriminated against? What faith this woman shows!" The Samaritan woman engages Jesus; she will not be dismissed. She is the one who runs to the village, tells her story to the people, and invites the people to meet Jesus face to face. She is the one without whom the self-revelation of Jesus would not have occurred. "It was clear to the Marburg group that Jesus revealed himself to the woman through their dialogue." She is the one who sees who he is. No, the role of the Samaritan woman in the story is crucial. It is not for nothing that she has become Haya Photini in the Orthodox tradition—the first evangelist, the bearer of the Holy Light.

Genuine sensitivity for the cultural codes operative in Mediterranean cultures is rarely found in the work of Western exegetes. The perspective of "culture" is one

---

12. A number of elements from John 4 return in the moving story of John 20 of the meeting between Jesus and another woman, Mary Magdalene.

of the most striking differences between how ordinary and professional readers approach the story of John 4. The list of examples is long and concerns elements like the strange meeting of a man and woman at that hour of day, the location of the meeting at Jacob's well in Joseph's field (ancestors/tradition; is Jesus the proto-ancestor?), the relationship between the villagers and the woman, the social position of the woman, the public vs. the private sphere, aspects of power, and collectivist elements in the story.

To give a single example, in verse 16 there is a remarkable narrative sequence. Jesus offers the woman an extremely tempting gift: living water, which she accepts immediately. She says, "Sir, give me this water so that I won't get thirsty and have to keep coming here to draw water." Instead of handing over the gift, Jesus now gives her an order: "Go, call your husband." Bultmann and many others say that this is merely a demonstration of Jesus' supernatural knowledge; he knew about the five men in her life. The group of Bolivian women who read this passage came up with a different answer: she had to call her husband to ask permission for Jesus to give her this gift! Such a discovery can be a gift to exegesis in prompting the question of whether this cultural code—i.e., that one must first know if a woman is married before one may, as a bachelor, offer her a gift—is also contained in this story.

The following dialogue poses a question to exegesis regarding phonetic aspects of the John 4 story. Two groups discussed the meaning of the question, "Will you give me a drink?" The Dutch group heard an arrogant, antifeminist, macho tone in verse 7. The Indian partner group, which held to a high Christology, disagreed with this interpretation entirely and gave two arguments: Jesus observes the conventions and does not ask any intimate questions; he could start with the intimate question about her five partners but does not do that. Second, "This [request] is understood as a polite request in the South Indian culture. The way it is said is important. The way the woman responded also indicates that it was polite enough and not a harsh command." From the Third Bank of the River the question is posed: Can the exegete mediate here?

Let me give one final example, again concerning the question with which it all begins: "Will you give me a drink?" Many groups and exegetes see this question as raising the problematic relationship between Jews and Samaritans, of course, but some do not see that it is of much interest for the interpretation of the rest of the story. Jesus is thirsty and asks for a drink. But groups who have to deal with racism or a caste system are immediately struck by this question. A Kwazulu Natal group said:

> One member explored further the idea of tradition, commenting that if the woman had used her container to give water to Jesus, she would have had to go back to her village without water, "*because the container would have to be ritually cleansed.*" This participant also argued that, ironically, though the disciples had gone off to buy food that was ritually clean, that same

food was now being prepared for them by the Samaritans" (my italics).

In another South African group, a woman remarked:

> I would like to begin with this event in Jesus' life where He asked water from the Samaritan woman. We see that she responded by saying how could He ask water from her because the Jews do not practice fellowship with the Samaritans. He had no right to ask water. Here we see the problem which we still have today—namely, *racism*. This is the old problem that people *do not want to eat together* (my italics).

Another participant in the same group agreed immediately:

> Even in old times it was there. This is what we see when Jesus asks for water—already then there was no fellowship, people did not use one another's food. She says Jesus has no right to ask water from her as a Samaritan woman. I agree that this text speaks about racism.

In India a participant from a group of untouchables responded with a remark that speaks not only to this verse but also to the relationship between Jesus and the disciples who watch from a distance and are not pleased: "In this well-advanced world, a high-class individual hardly dares to extend a hand of friendship to the downtrodden. Suppose, say, it is done, then that individual has to confront many problems from his fellow beings (his own people)." Finally, yet another commentator, a transsexual also from India, stated about verse 6:

> She has a very hostile air about her and flippantly, though sounding very concerned, asks how Christ would be able to get water because he didn't even have buckets or jugs. There could have been two reasons for this—either the Jews *would rather go thirsty than touch the vessels of a Samaritan,* or she didn't want to help" (my italics).

This last example also seems to me to be a beautiful gift from the Third Bank of the River to exegetes and translators. Can it be that the question with which this conversation begins is in fact one that is extremely disconcerting and transgresses boundaries? Does it place us in the sociocultural domain of racism, where class and caste differences are felt most profoundly and in their most degrading ways—where the other is seen as disgusting, dirty, and impure? Can it be that Jesus in fact says to the woman, "If you want to accept from me that I am prepared to step across the boundary of impurity, are you prepared to meet me, and will you give me your 'impure' jar?"

The exegetes' task is clear. The translators should check whether the translation of the verb *sunchraomai* in the commentary in verse 9—"For Jews do not associate with Samaritans" (NIV)—should be replaced by what is found, for instance, in the *Naardense Bijbel* and other Dutch versions: "For Judeans/Jews do not use anything together with Samaritans."

We will leave our examples at that. I hope that I have made it clear how special the gift of the popular reading of the Bible can be to the exegete. And by *gift*, I do mean gift. What is given by ordinary readers to professional ones is not only an idea—an insight into the text that must now be validated. No, a hierarchical relationship would neglect too much the character of exegesis as play and would continue to give preference to only one way of playing. The gift that is given has to do with the importance of the unfamiliar—the introduction of experiences that are often foreign to Western exegetes but are nevertheless found in the texts, if one looks for them. It is a gift that enriches exegesis, making it less abstract and freer with respect to dominant reading traditions and the requirements of the fraternity, and enabling this discipline to assume its ethical responsibility.

9

The Ordinary Reader Revisited

In this research project, practice and the formation of theory are focused on the ordinary readers to whom we just listened. The "ordinary reader" is more than a flesh-and-blood reader—it represents an attitude toward the text, defined by Paul Ricoeur as the existential attitude. It is the space in which the effect of Holy Scripture is evident. It is a dynamic playing field in which Bible texts are not soiled but called into new life; a field where a gigantic reservoir of experiences and memories, of social memory, becomes clear; and a space that reflects asymmetry, challenging us to give an ethical answer. Viewed from the often closed world of exegesis, this space has to do with an elsewhere, an otherwise, and the "other." In it, the value of the unfamiliar and foreign, and the voices that have been pushed aside, manifest themselves. Exegetes who want to enter this space are boundary crossers.

I hope that I have indicated the importance of this space for biblical studies, theology, and translators of the Bible. If the discussion on rights and justice, on asymmetry, and on what faith has to do with all of this is shown clearly in a fundamental way in this space of intercultural Bible reading, then there is more than sufficient reason for churches, missions, and even development organizations to enter it.

10

Intercultural Bible Reading as Missionary Strategy

In Lambert Hoedemaker's (2000) book, *Met anderen tot Christus: Zending in een postmissionair tijdperk* (With Others to Christ: Mission in a Postmissionary Age), I find arguments for seeing intercultural Bible reading as a new practice, as a missionary strategy that answers challenges presented to missiology. Hoedemaker attempts to look critically at missiological thinking in the last decades. By the term *postmissionary,* Hoedemaker means a new period marked by deep asymmetry on one hand and worldwide secularization versus religious pluralism on the other. It is a period in which classical missionary thinking is faced with immense challenges. In particular, more evangelical views of missions have few answers to these challenges. According to Hoedemaker, all kinds of core concepts of mission must be fundamentally rethought. Classical insular Western thinking on missions has too often been "exile missiology," a missiology of the isolated West. In contemporary missiological thinking, globalization, pluralism, and inequality must be given a place.

To that end, Hoedemaker latches onto a classic core term of missiology, which also plays an important role in our argument: its eschatological character. According to Hoedemaker, the problems of the postmissionary age have an eschatological structure: pluralism, globalization, contextuality, and culture. These are movements and phenomena that bear in themselves references to and longings for something else, something new: finally a redeemed and liberated humanity, a deep and complete mutual acknowledgement among people, and a successful communication in which all of humankind is involved—"reconciled variety." "Mission" by the Christian church has always meant that one reaches in the world from the "dangerous memory" to the world of the eschaton. To speak about "reconciled difference" is to hold on to the perspective that knows and transcends the isolation of particular contexts, to a unity that goes deeper than the façade of the unity of globalization and offsets the destructive aspects of plurality.

As long as difference could be perceived and named on the basis of the existing "unity" that was perceived as normative, it was much less necessary to speak about "reconciled difference," according to Hoedemaker. But now Christians, and certainly Western Christians, can no longer survey difference at a removed distance from a presumed normative perspective. And this fact has tremendous implications for thinking about missions. "Mission" must be convinced of the fact that Christians are found in the midst of other Christians and communities that, like themselves, make and maintain traditions around the "signs" they receive with respect to salvation and redemption.

The fact that the normative "orthodoxy" of Christianity has become problematic suggests that we need to look differently at faith and also at mission. Hoedemaker writes, "The Christian faith is not a ready system of meanings that only has to include the 'world' to the degree to which the believers bring their 'worlds' into it and thus arrange and rearrange the system." The Christian faith and the Christian tradition are deeply hermeneutical and are themselves a conversation—a permanent interaction directed at the "end," at reconciliation and redemption. What happens "contextually" and "in dialogue" contributes via its content to the formation of the tradition.

All of this means that the "other" is essential for the discussion on faith. This discussion must not be like interrogating a prisoner, to use Gadamer's image again, as in some evangelical views of missions in which the importance of the discussion with the other is underestimated time and again. In any case, this discussion should have two components. On the one hand is the retrieval of the learning moments in one's own tradition and Scripture. On the other hand is the analysis of the "oneness of humanity" problem—keeping open the critical questions that must be asked in that analysis and remaining focused on an eschaton that reaches beyond what humanity can actually achieve. Gauges for this can be participation (in movements for change), prophetic criticism (being moved by the *humanum*), and missions as service (listening) within the framework of reconciliation (plurality).

We will leave our discussion of Hoedemaker's insights at that. If we place these insights next to current missions practice, the question quickly arises whether our thinking on mission is not unconsciously still and strongly directed at the people and places "out there," while we ourselves and the organizational structure remain unaffected. The remarkable paradox comes to light: the more we occupy ourselves with organizational structure, with validating the results of projects, with solutions to problems between church and church, the less time we have to actually increase cultural sensitivity in a truly missionary sense, to initiate new mission practices, and to supervise them and learn from them.

How much actual conversation occurs with the "other" elsewhere on the grassroots level of our churches? Do we have any idea? The African Musimbi Kanyoro finds, "Relations between church and church are much too oriented to solving problems and too little to dialogue, discussion, and a joint process." Instead of solving problems, she believes that people should strengthen the hope that is present. She uses the image of a pregnant woman who climbs a tree during the floods in Mozambique, is forced to stay there for five days, and gives birth to a child high above the flood.

Perhaps we should indeed begin to think about missionary relationships in that way. Intercultural Bible reading can then be seen as a new missionary practice that is related critically to institutionalized practices and attempts to do justice to the eschatological dimension of missions. It is not officials who are the mediators of mission strategies but ordinary believers. Our empirical material shows that a new separate missionary agenda does not have to be conceived for this new practice but is itself an agenda. The empirical material convinces us that the intercultural discussion on the meaning of Bible stories does not lead to an aimless conversation but is constantly missiologically laden. As such, it is a fundamental source for missionary renewal. Perhaps then, high above both banks of the flooded river—in the tree of which Musimbi Kanyoro speaks—our boat in the time of cholera can be the place where a child is born.

11

Intercultural Bible Reading as Development Strategy

That the joint, intercultural reading of the Bible could contribute as a development strategy will sound strange to many. Before explaining this concept, I would like to say that it surprises me that it has not been done before. The fact that the Bible has seldom been involved in reflection on development is astonishing for two simple reasons: first, despite processes of secularization in the Two-Thirds World, religion is still very much a part of that world; and second, for the (Christian) religious universe, the Bible is the most important compass.

What holds true for ordinary believers also holds true for development organizations that want to give (the Christian) religion a role in their search for their identity and policy; they appeal to ethical-religious traditions. The ways they use those sources clarify how they articulate their identity, operationalize it, and make it relevant. However, Christian-oriented development organizations cannot authentically and responsibly make these traditions relevant without discussion with the "other" in the Two-Thirds World whom they wish to serve. The "other" in the Two-Thirds World, this particular epiphanic space, not only often lives and dies in circumstances that go beyond any Western ability to imagine but also often is rooted in—from a secularized Western perspective—a remarkably deep and immediate way in the same ethical-religious tradition. Often, it is this tradition that, more than any secular worldview, offers a person space to survive in a situation of contrast experiences. The price that the development organizations pay for neglecting or ignoring what is of fundamental importance for the other is high; the other is instrumentalized and reduced to what the secularized, Western perspective will accept. While we lack the room to examine this issue more closely here, I do believe that the space in which the discussion on faith occurs can be fruitful for development policy. I am thinking here of some concrete matters.

The demonic dilemma of all development work can be eased. I am referring here to the dilemma that exists when development organizations reduce the people they wish to serve—those from the global South—to only one aspect of their existence to be able to help them: their hunger, disease, or poverty. Such reduction ceases when stories from the people's immediate life situations become visible. Rather than offering a helicopter view, these life stories zoom in on the people's contexts and their concrete experiences, offering an insider's perspective. If development organizations want to have an insider's perspective on the effects of underdevelopment and poverty, they should look carefully at such stories—not simply at the misery but also at the dreams, power, and hope that people derive from the biblical story in situations of obvious suffering.

In the space of intercultural hermeneutics, Western groups can participate wholeheartedly. Because of this factor, "the discussion with the poor" is not limited to the small circle of policy advisers. Not only do the rich talk with the poor, but it also appears that they can share each other's resistance, struggles, and tears. According to the biblical scholar Jobling, "sites of struggle that are not only invisible to each other but that might not even be recognized by each other as sites of struggle" become mutually visible.

Resourcing is actively pursued in the space of intercultural hermeneutics. Through reading the Bible together, small interpretive communities can contribute in a modest yet fundamental way to the process of identity formation. Thus, religious intercourse can also place dominant development paradigms under criticism. Religious insights and beliefs also can be explored with respect to their capacity to function as critical criteria for evaluating development models.

12

When Love Again Has a Master

While the *Nueva Fidelidad,* the New Fidelity, is sailing over the river and will shortly have no other destination than to nourish love, Florentino is in Fermina's cabin. Apart from the ice-cold hand, there has been no other contact so far.

> [Fermina] felt untroubled and calm, as she had few times in her life: free of all blame. She would have remained there until dawn, silent, with his hand perspiring ice into hers, but she could not endure the torment in her ear. . . . She realized that her pain was stronger than her desire to be with him. She knew that telling him about it would alleviate her suffering, but she did not because she did not want to worry him. For now it seemed to her that she knew him as well as if she had lived with him all her life, and she thought him capable of ordering the boat back to port if that would relieve her pain.
>
> Florentino had foreseen how things would be that night, and he withdrew. At the door of her cabin he tried to kiss her good night, but she offered him her left cheek. He insisted, with labored breath, and she offered him her other cheek, with a coquettishness that he had not known when she was a schoolgirl. Then he insisted again, and she offered him her lips, she offered her lips with a profound trembling that she tried to suppress with the laugh she had forgotten after her wedding night.
>
> "My God," she said, "ships make me so crazy." (García Márquez 1989, 334–35)

On the final day of the return journey, they wake up at six o'clock. The decision to make the destiny of the boat nothing else than to serve love has not yet been made. The idea that the trip is now at an end and that everyone must now return to his or her own bank of the river turns their stomachs.

> "It's going to be like dying," she said.
> Florentino Ariza was startled, because her words read a thought that had given him no peace since the beginning of the voyage home. Neither one could imagine being in any other home but the cabin, or eating in any other way but on the ship, or living any other life, for that would be alien to them forever. It was, indeed, like dying. (346)

The story of the meeting on the boat and that of the meeting at the well show striking parallels. Jesus and the Samaritan woman do unusual things as well. The disciples, who are not anywhere near or happy about anything—and do not accept her either—see it. They find Jesus' behavior at the well very strange. When they come back from buying food, they "are surprised to find him talking with a woman. But no one asked, 'What do you want?' or 'Why are you talking with her?'" (v. 27). But she also does unusual things; she undergoes a radical transformation—she, who had gone to the well alone at that hour, avoided by everyone and avoiding everyone. It is as if she has lost it. She leaves her jar—many groups say her past—behind; she runs back to her family, the villagers, and like a bride who has just met her bridegroom, says to them, "Come, see a man who told me everything I ever did."

A few factors are crucial, apparently, for profound encounters that transcend boundaries: vulnerability, the masks that fall away, a third place—we have discussed them extensively. But the most crucial is the small gesture of love: the understanding that there is no other place where our capacity for love can blossom than the other, ensuring that love once again has a master. The small gesture of love, the hand that lies ready, a question that is posed or, in the words of Câmara himself: "a glance, a gesture of peace and friendship, a smile."

It is remarkable how seldom people laugh in our discussions about multicultural society. Whether we want to or not, most of us are riding on the boat as well. I hope that the practice of reading sacred texts together will allow us to experience and to witness the power of such small gestures of love.

The Smile at the Well, by Hari Santosa (Indonesia)

References

Aalbersberg–van Loon, C. 2003. *De derde stem en de vierde stem: een onderzoek naar het functioneren van Psalm 31 en 139 in het pastoraat.* Kampen: Kok.

Adamo, David Tuesday. 1999. "African Cultural Hermeneutics." In *Vernacular Hermeneutics,* edited by R. S. Surgirtharajah, 66–91. Sheffield: Sheffield Academic Press.

Aldunate, José. 2008. "Una Encuesta Inquietante sobre el Catolicismo Chileno." *Pastoral Popular* 47, no. 308: 22–23.

Althusser, Louis. 1972. *Lenin and Philosophy, and Other Essays.* New York: Monthly Review Press.

Attridge, Harold W., and Margot E. Fassler, eds. 2003. *Psalms in Community: Jewish and Christian Textual, Liturgical, and Artistic Traditions.* Society of Biblical Literature Symposium Series 25. Atlanta: Society of Biblical Literature.

Bahloul, Joëlle. 2002. *Lecturas Precarias: Estudio sociológico sobre los "poco lectores."* Mexico: Fondo de Cultura. Originally published as *Lectures précaires: étude sociologique sur les faible lecteurs* (Paris: BPI Centre Pompidou, 1998).

Bal, Mieke. 1990. *De theorie van vertellen en verhalen.* Muideberg: Coutinho.

Bar-Tal, Daniel. 1990. "Israel-Palestinian Conflict: A Cognitive Analysis." *International Journal of Intercultural Relations* 14: 7–29.

Bleich, David. 1988. *The Double Perspective: Language, Literacy, and Social Relations.* New York: Oxford University Press.

Blount, B. K. 1995. *Cultural Interpretation: Reorienting New Testament Criticism.* Minneapolis: Fortress.

Boff, Clodovis. 1980. *Teología de lo Político: Sus Mediaciones.* Salamanca: Sígueme.

Câmara, Hélder. 1969. *Revolutie in Vredesnamm.* Utrecht: Bruna. Originally published as *Revolução dentro da Paz* (Rio de Janeiro: Sabia, 1968). Citations refer to the Dutch edition.

———. 1971. *Spirale de Violence.* Brussels: Desclée de Broucker. Also published as *Spiral of Violence* (London: Sheed and Ward, 1971).

———. 1972. Message to the Mani Tese [Outstretched Hands] youth movement, at the climax of its 1972 march, Plaza Michelangelo, Florence, Italy, November 7, 1972. Published in *Hélder Câmara: Proclamas a la Juventud,* Serie PEDAL 64, edited by Benedicto Tapia de Renedo, 199–204 (Salamanca: Ediciones Sígueme, 1976).

Cohn Eskenazi, Tamara. 2003. "Love Your Neighbor as an Other: Reflections on Levinas's Ethics and the Hebrew Bible." In *Levinas and Biblical Studies,* Semeia Studies 43, edited by Tamara Cohn Eskenazi, Gary Phillips, and David Jobling, 145–58. Atlanta: Society of Biblical Literature.

————, Gary Phillips, and David Jobling, eds. 2003. *Levinas and Biblical Studies.* Semeia Studies 43. Atlanta: Society of Biblical Literature.

de Wit, J. H. 1991. *Leerlingen van de Armen.* Amsterdam: VU Uitgeverij.

————. 2000. "Leyendo con Yael: Un ejercicio en hermenéutica intercultural." In *Los caminos inexhauribles de la Palabra (las relecturas creativas en la biblia y de la biblia): homenaje de colegas y discípulos a J. Severino Croatto,* edited by Guillermo Hansen, 11–66. Buenos Aires: Lumen.

————. 2001. "Lezen met Jael: Op weg naar interculturele hermeneutick." *Amsterdamse Cahiers voor Exegese van de Bijbel en zijn Tradities* 19: 71–96.

————. 2004a. "Codes and Coding." In *Through the Eyes of Another: Intercultural Reading of the Bible,* edited by Hans de Wit et al., 395–436. Elkhart, IN: Institute of Mennonite Studies.

————. 2004b. "Intercultural Bible Reading and Hermeneutics." In *Through the Eyes of Another: Intercultural Reading of the Bible,* edited by Hans de Wit et al., 477–92. Elkhart, IN: Institute of Mennonite Studies.

————. 2004c. "Through the Eyes of Another: Objectives and Backgrounds." In *Through the Eyes of Another: Intercultural Reading of the Bible,* edited by Hans de Wit et al., 3–53. Elkhart, IN: Institute of Mennonite Studies.

————. 2006a. "Caminho dum dia' (Jonas 3.4): Jonas e a memoria social dos pequenos." In *Profecia e esperança: um tributo a Milton Schwantes,* edited by Carlos A. Dreher. São Leopoldo: Oikos.

————. 2006b. "Latin American Hermeneutics of Liberation—From Conversion to Conviction. In *Mezinárodní symposium o teologii osvobození,* edited by Mical Cáb, Roman Mícka, and Marek Pelech, 44–57. Ceské Budejovice: Teologická fakulta Jihocedské Universzity.

————. 2008. "Exegesis and Contextuality: Happy Marriage, Divorce or Living (Apart) Together?" In *African and European Readers of the Bible in Dialgue: In Quest of a Shared Meaning,* edited by Hans de Wit and Gerald O. West, 7–26. Leiden: Brill.

Droogers, André. 2006. *Het gedwongen huwelijk russen Vrouwe Religie en Heer Macht.* Amsterdam: VU Uitgeverij.

Dyk, Janet. 2004a. "Levend Water: wonderbaarlijke woorden van leven." In *Putten uit de Bron: Een bijbelverhaal intercultureel gelezen,* edited by Hans de Wit et al., 218–42. Zoetermeer: Meinema.

————. 2004b. "Living Water: Wonderful Words of Life." In *Through the Eyes of Another: Intercultural Reading of the Bible,* edited by Hans de Wit et al., 377–94. Elkhart, IN: Institute of Mennonite Studies.

Eagleton, Terry. 1976. *Criticism and Ideology: A Study in Marxist Literary Theory.* London: NLB.

Eco, Umberto. 1991. "De tekst, het leesgenot, de consumptie." In *Wat spiegels betreft: Essays,* 107ff. Amsterdam: Bakker. Originally published as *Sugli specchi e altri saggi* (Milan: Bompiani, 1985).

————. 1997. *Kant e l'ornitorinco.* Milano: Bompiani.

Fish, Stanley. 1980. *Is There a Text in this Class? The Authority of Interpretive Communities*. Cambridge: Harvard University Press.

Fishbane, Michael A. 1985. *Biblical Interpretation in Ancient Israel*. Oxford: Clarendon Press.

Frei, Hans W. 1974. *The Eclipse of Biblical Narrative: A Study in Eighteenth and Nineteenth Century Hermeneutics*. New Haven: Yale University Press.

Gadamer, Hans-Georg. 1986. "Hermeneutik als theoretische und praktische Aufgabe." In *Wahrheit und Methode: Ergänzungen*. Gesammelte Werke Band 2. Tübingen: Mohr.

———. 1990. *Wahrheit und Methode: Grundzüge einer philosophischen Hermeneutik*. Tübingen: Mohr.

Ganzevoort, Ruard R. 2005. "Als de grondslagen vernield zign: Religie, trauma en pastoraat." *Praktische Theologie* 32, no. 3: 344–61.

García Márquez, Gabriel. 1989. *Love in the Time of Cholera*, translated by Edith Grossman. London: Penguin. Originally published as *El Amor en los Tiempos del Cólera* (Bogota: Editorial Oveja Negra, 1985). Unless otherwise indicated, citations refer to the Penguin edition.

Glaser, Barney G. 1993. *Examples of Grounded Theory: A Reader*. Mill Valley, CA: Sociology Press.

———, and Anselm L. Strauss 1967. *The Discovery of Grounded Theory: Strategies for Qualitative Research*. Chicago: Aldine Publishing Co.

Halbwachs, Maurice. 1980. *The Collective Memory*. New York: Harper & Row. Originally published as *La Mémoire Collective* (Paris: Presses universitaires de France, 1950).

Hand, Seán, ed. 1989. *The Levinas Reader*. Oxford: Blackwell.

Heijst, Annelies van. 1992. *Verlangen naar de Val*. Kampen: Kok Agora.

Heitink, Gerben. 2001. *Biografie van de Dominee*. Baarn: Ten Have.

Hoedemaker, L. A. 2000. *Met anderen tot Christus: Zending in een postmissionair tijdperk*. Zoetermeer: Boekencentrum.

Hoekema, Aukje. 2004. "Het begrip 'heil' in Johannes 4:22: Getekenisverschillen door alle groepen heen." In *Putten uit de Bron: Een bijbelverhaal intercultureel gelezen*, edited by Hans de Wit et al., 171–88. Zoetermeer: Meinema.

Huggan, Graham. 2001. *The Postcolonial Exotic: Marketing the Margins*. London: Routledge.

Huning, Ralf. 2005. *Bibelwissenschaft im Dienste popularer Bibellektüre: Bausteine einer Theorie der Bibellektüre aus dem Werk von Carlos Mesters*. Stuttgart: Verl. Kath. Bibelwerk.

Irwin-Zarecka, Iwona. 1994. *Frames of Remembrance: The Dynamics of Collective Memory*. New Brunswick, NJ: Transaction Publishers.

Jauss, Hans Robert. 1982. *Towards an Aesthetic of Reception*. Minneapolis: University of Minnesota Press.

Keightly, G. M. 2005. "Christian Collective Memory and Paul's Knowledge of Jesus." In *Memory, Tradition, and Text: Uses of the Past in Early*

Christianity, Semeia Studies 52, edited by Alan Kirk and Tom Thatcher, 129–50. Atlanta: Society of Biblical Literature.

Kirk, Alan. 2005. "Social and Cultural Memory: Introduction." In *Memory, Tradition, and Text: Uses of the Past in Early Christianity,* Semeia Studies 52, edited by Alan Kirk and Tom Thatcher, 1–24. Atlanta: Society of Biblical Literature.

————, and Tom Thatcher, eds. 2005. *Memory, Tradition, and Text: Uses of the Past in Early Christianity.* Semeia Studies 52. Atlanta: Society of Biblical Literature.

Kohler Riessman, Catherine. 2002. "Narrative Analysis." In *The Qualitative Researcher's Companion,* edited by A. Michael Huberman and Matthew B. Miles, 217–70. Thousand Oaks, CA: Sage Publications.

Koster, Edwin. 2005. *In Betovering Gevangen: Over verhaal en rationaliteit, religie en irrationaliteit.* Budel: Uitgeverij DAMON.

Labberton, Mark.1990. *Ordinary Bible Reading: The Reformed Tradition and Reader-Oriented Criticism.* Cambridge: University of Cambridge.

Levinas, Emmanuel. 1961. *Totalité et infini: Essai sur l'exteriorité.* The Hague: Nijhoff. Published in English translation as *Totality and Infinity: An Essay on Exteriority,* translated by Alphonso Lingis (Pittsburgh: Duquesne University Press, 1961).

————. 1989. "Revelation in Jewish Tradition." In *The Levinas Reader,* edited by Seán Hand, 159ff. Oxford: Blackwell.

Malina, Bruce. 1983. "The Social Sciences and Biblical Interpretation." In *The Bible and Liberation: Political and Social Hermeneutics,* edited by N. K. Gottwald, 11–25. Maryknoll: Orbis Books.

McGovern, Arthur F. 1990. *Liberation Theology and Its Critics: Toward an Assessment.* Maryknoll: Orbis Books.

Míguez Bonino, José. 2002. "Love and Social Transformation." In *The Promise of Hope: A Tribute to Dom Hélder,* edited by Daniel S. Schipani and Anton Wessels, 88–104. Elkhart, IN: Institute of Mennonite Studies.

Namer, Gérard. 1987. *Mémoire et société.* Paris: Méridiens Klincksieck.

O'Connor, Mark. "Dom Hélder: A Mystic in Love with the Poor." Unpublished eulogy.

Paas, Marianne. 2004. "Zien en gezien worden." In *Putten uit de Bron: Een bijbelverhaal intercultureel gelezen,* edited by Hans de Wit et al., 89–95. Zoetermeer: Meinema.

Phillips, Gary A. 1994. "The Ethics of Reading Deconstructively, or Speaking Face-to-Face: The Samaritan Woman Meets Derrida at the Well." In *The New Literary Criticism and the New Testament, Journal for the Study of the New Testament, Supplement Series 109,* edited by Elizabeth Struthers Malbon and Edgar V. Knight, 283–325. Sheffield: Sheffield Academic Press.

Procee, Hendrik. 1991. *Over de Grenzen van Culturen.* Amsterdam: Contact Uitgeverij.

Richard, Pablo. 1982. "La Biblia, Memoria histórica de los Pobres." *Servir* 18, no. 98: 143–50. Also published in Portuguese as "Bíblia: Memoria Histórica dos Pobres," *Estudos Bíblicos* 1 (1987): 20–30.

Ricoeur, Paul. 1984. *The Reality of the Historical Past.* Milwaukee: Marquette University Press.

———. 1998. "Preface." In *Thinking Biblically: Exegetical and Hermeneutical Studies,* by A. Lacocque and P. Ricoeur, translated by David Pellauer, ix–xix. Chicago: University of Chicago Press.

Sanford, A. J., and S. C. Garrod. 1981. *Understanding Written Language.* Chichester: John Wiley & Sons.

Schipani, Daniel S., and Anton Wessels, eds. 2002. *The Promise of Hope: A Tribute to Dom Hélder.* Elkhart IN: Institute of Mennonite Studies.

Schnackenburg, Rudolf. 1972. *Das Johannesevangelium.* Herders Theologischer Kommentar zum Neuen Testament 4, 1. Freiburg: Herder.

Schreiter, Robert J. 1997. *The New Catholicity: Theology between the Global and the Local.* Maryknoll: Orbis Books.

Schwantes, Milton. 1987. "Nuestra Vista Clareó: Lectura Bíblica en América Latina." *Presencia Ecuménica* 7:3–9.

Scott, James C. 1990. *Domination and the Arts of Resistance: Hidden Transcripts.* New Haven: Yale University Press.

Severino Croatto, José. 1982. "Una promesa aun no cumplida: Algunos enfoques sobre la estructura literaria del Pentateuco." *Revista Bíblica* 44: 193ff.

———. 1991. Cómo releer la Biblia desde su contexto socio-político? Ejercicio sobre algunos temas del Pentateuco." *Revista Bíblica* 53/44: 193–212.

———. 1994. "Exodo 1–15: Algunas Claves literarias y teológicas para entender el pentateuco." *Estudios Bíblicos* 52: 167–94.

———. 1997. *Exilio y Sobrevivencia: Tradiciones contraculturales en el Pentateuco.* Buenos Aires: Lumen.

Smith, W. C. 1993. *What Is Scripture?* London: SCM Press Ltd.

Snoek, Hans. 2004. "Deelnemers en Wetenschappers in gesprek over levend water: Overeenkomsten en verschillen in wijze van benaderen." In *Putten uit de Bron: Een bijbelverhaal intercultureel gelezen,* edited by Hans de Wit et al., 189–201. Zoetermeer: Meinema.

Thiselton, Anthony C. 1992. *New Horizons in Hermeneutics: The Theory and Practice of Transforming Biblical Reading.* Grand Rapids: Zondervan.

Trible, Phyllis. 1984. *Texts of Terror: Literary-Feminist Readings of Biblical Narratives.* Philadelphia: Fortress.

Ukpong, Justin. 2000. "Popular Reading of the Bible." In *The Bible in Africa,* edited by Gerald O. West and Musa W. Dube, 582–94. Leiden: Brill.

Vander Stichele, Carolyn. 2005. "Introduction." In *Her Master's Tools? Feminist and Postcolonial Engagements of Historical-Critical Discourse,*

Global Perspectives on Biblical Scholarship 9, edited by Caroline Vander Stichele and Todd Penner, 10ff. Atlanta: Society of Biblical Literature.

van der Ven, Johannes A. 1994. *Entwurf einer empirischen Theologie.* Kampen: Kok.

Vanheste, Bert. 1981. *Literatuursociologie: Theorie en Methode.* Assen: Van Gorcum.

van Nieuwenhove, J. 1991. *Bronnen van Bevrijding: Varianten in de theologie van Gustavo Gutiérrez.* Kampen: Kok.

van Veldhuizen, Piet. 2004. *Geef mij te drinken: Johannes 4, 4–42 als waterputverhaal.* Zoetermeer: Boekencentrum.

Vogel, Marianne. 2001. *"Baard boven baard": Over het Nederlandse literaire en maatschappelijke leven 1945–1960.* Amsterdam: Van Gennep.

West, Gerald O. 1993. "No Integrity without Contextuality: The Presence of Particularity in Biblical Hermeneutics and Pedagogy." *Scriptura* S11: 131–46.

———. 1996. "Reading the Bible Differently: Giving Shape to the Discourse of the Dominated." *Semeia: An Experimental Journal for Biblical Criticism* 73: 21–41.

———. 1997. "On the Eve of an African Biblical Studies: Trajectories and Trends." *Journal of Theology for Southern Africa* 99: 99–115.

———. 1999. *The Academy of the Poor: Towards a Dialogical Reading of the Bible.* Sheffield: Sheffield Academic Press.

———. 2000. "Mapping African Biblical Interpretation: A Tentative Sketch." In *The Bible in Africa: Transactions, Trajectories and Trends,* edited by Gerald O. West and Musa W. Dube, 29–53. Leiden: Brill.

———, and Musa W. Dube, editors. 1996. "'Reading With': An Exploration of the Interface between Critical and Ordinary Readings of the Bible: African Overtures." *Semeia: An Experimental Journal for Biblical Criticism* 73.

The Author

Dr. Hans (J. H.) de Wit is professor at the Faculty of Theology, VU University Amsterdam, The Netherlands. Dr. de Wit studied theology at VU University Amsterdam and specialized in the field of Old Testament. From 1980 to 1989 he worked in Chile, Latin America, at the Comunidad Teológica Evangélica de Chile as professor of Old Testament and Biblical Hermeneutics.

In his dissertation, *Leerlingen van de Armen* (Pupils of the Poor), 1991, de Wit analyzes the so-called Latin American Biblical Movement and the interface between exegesis and "ordinary reading" (*lectura popular*) of the Bible.

De Wit has lectured in India, South Africa, Germany, Hungary, and Latin American countries including Argentina, Brazil, Cuba, Costa Rica, Nicaragua, Colombia, Ecuador, and Puerto Rico. De Wit is one of the initiators of a new international project called Through the Eyes of Another: Intercultural Reading of the Bible. At the present intercultural (biblical) hermeneutics is one of Hans de Wit's fields of interest. He is the author of numerous essays published in journals and books. Books for which he has served as author or editor include *En la dispersión el texto es Patria: Introducción a la hermenéutica clásica, moderna y posmoderna* (2002); *Por un solo gesto de amor: Lectura de la Biblia desde una practica intercultural* (2010); *Putten uit de Bron: Een bijbelverhaal intercultureel gelezen* (2004); *Through the Eyes of Another: Intercultural Reading of the Bible* (2004); and *African and European Readers of the Bible in Dialogue: In Quest of a Shared Meaning* (2008).

Since October 2007, Dr. de Wit is holder of the Dom Hélder Câmara chair for liberation and peace at VU University Amsterdam.